Unmasking the Gilgo beach Serial Killer

A Chilling True Crime Story of Murder, Mystery, and the Relentless Pursuit of Justice

Adriana O. Babs

Table of contents

Introduction

Uncovering Long Island's Dark Mystery

The Long Island coastline has always held a unique allure. From summer vacations to quiet walks along the sand, it's a place where countless families, couples, and individuals find solace in the simple rhythm of ocean waves against the shore. But in December 2010, the calm beauty of Long Island was disrupted in the most haunting way. The discovery of human remains near Gilgo Beach would set off an investigation that would span years, exposing a disturbing mystery lurking within the shadows of an otherwise serene place. This mystery would come to be known as the Gilgo Beach murders, forever tainting the quiet beauty of the area with a history too chilling to forget.

The Gilgo Beach murders not only shook the local community but also captured the nation's attention. The case spoke to the darkest aspects of human behaviour, highlighting the vulnerabilities of those living on the margins, and exposing the terrifying reality that monsters can hide in plain sight. This was not merely a local tragedy; it was a wake-up call that resonated far and wide, casting a spotlight on the weaknesses within our justice system and on the societal factors that made these crimes possible.

Setting the Scene at Gilgo Beach

Gilgo Beach, with its sandy stretches and breezy air, was an unassuming backdrop for such a horrific discovery. Located on the south shore of Long Island, New York, it's part of a series of beaches that have attracted locals and tourists for years. But in 2010, it became synonymous with something far darker. When authorities uncovered the first of what would become many bodies along Ocean Parkway, the reality of a serial killer's presence shattered the tranquillity of this otherwise peaceful region. The remains were found in an isolated, almost abandoned part of the area, an eerily fitting locale for such a grim find.

In May 2010, Shannan Gilbert, a young woman in her twenties, went missing after a late-night 911 call in which she sounded terrified, as though running for her life. Her disappearance led police to search the marshy areas around Gilgo Beach. What began as a hunt for one missing person rapidly spiralled into a full-fledged investigation into multiple unsolved murders.

Within months of beginning the search for Shannan, the authorities stumbled upon the remains of several other young women, each buried in shallow graves or left along the same desolate stretch of beach. These women were later identified as sex workers who had gone missing in the years prior. The discovery of their bodies in such proximity raised the unnerving question: had a serial killer been operating undetected on Long Island, preying on vulnerable women and leaving their bodies in plain sight?

The Discovery of the First Bodies

The bodies were not found all at once; rather, they were unearthed gradually, each discovery adding a new layer of horror to an already gruesome narrative. The first four victims were found within a week of each other in December 2010. As the investigation progressed, more bodies emerged, and the number of victims increased, encompassing both identified and unidentified individuals. Law enforcement officials, who initially hoped this would be an isolated case, now faced the grim reality that they were dealing with something far larger and more sinister than they had anticipated.

What followed was a painstaking investigation as authorities combed through the sandy terrain, analysing every inch of the area. The bodies showed signs of deliberate concealment, indicating the killer had taken steps to ensure their crimes went undetected for as long as possible. Many of the remains were skeletal, suggesting they had been left for years, yet others were more recent, indicating the possibility that the killer had been active up until very recently. For a community unaccustomed to such violence, this was a horrific shock. People began to lock their doors, talk about "the beach" in hushed tones, and worry about what other dark secrets Long Island might be hiding.

As law enforcement dug deeper, so did the media. The discovery of multiple bodies in such close proximity on a tranquil beach became a story that was impossible to ignore. News stations flocked to the scene, reporters delved into the lives of the victims, and the public watched in horror as new details emerged about the lives lost and the slow pace of the investigation.

The Shockwaves Across the Community

For the people of Long Island, this was not just a crime — it was a profound betrayal of the security and safety they had once felt in their community. The Gilgo Beach murders cast a long shadow over Long

Island, leaving the community reeling and grappling with the enormity of what had happened in their backyard. The knowledge that a serial killer had been using their home as a dumping ground left residents uneasy, mistrustful, and forever changed.

Families of the victims were thrust into the media spotlight, some of them learning only now the horrifying fates of their loved ones. These were mothers, daughters, and sisters who had lived under the uncertainty of not knowing, year after year, what had happened to the ones they loved. The confirmation of their deaths brought closure but also a fresh wound, compounded by the brutal way in which they were taken. These families became symbols of resilience and determination as they demanded answers, often frustrated by the slow-moving investigation and the media's portrayal of their loved ones as little more than victims of a serial killer.

Meanwhile, the local authorities faced mounting pressure to bring justice to the victims and assurance to the community. The public demanded answers, and the media relentlessly scrutinised every step of the investigation. Detectives and officials on the case worked tirelessly, but the complexity of the investigation, combined with the years that had passed since some of the murders, meant that progress was slow and often frustratingly inconclusive. The killer, whoever they were, seemed to have vanished without a trace, leaving behind nothing but heartbreak and questions.

The shockwaves extended beyond Long Island, reaching across the country and even beyond. The Gilgo Beach murders became a stark reminder of the vulnerabilities faced by people on the margins of society — the invisible, the forgotten, and the silenced. It also forced society to confront uncomfortable truths about the dangers that can lie just beneath the surface, hiding in plain sight within our communities.

Purpose of This Book: Understanding the Story, the Victims, and the Hunt for Justice

This book seeks to do more than recount the grim facts of the Gilgo Beach murders. It is a journey through the lives of the victims, the complexities of the investigation, and the emotional toll on those left behind. We will explore the histories of these women, examining who they were beyond the tragic labels the media has so often assigned them. By sharing their stories, we hope to bring a sense of humanity to the narrative, reminding readers that these were real people, each with dreams, struggles, and loved ones who continue to mourn their loss.

Furthermore, this book seeks to shed light on the frustratingly slow process of bringing a serial killer to justice. From the initial discovery of bodies to the recent arrest of Rex Heuermann, we will follow the twists and turns of the investigation, exploring the breakthroughs and setbacks that defined the hunt for the Gilgo Beach killer. The story of this investigation is also a story about resilience — of families who refused to give up, of law enforcement officials who worked tirelessly despite the odds, and of a community that had to learn how to cope with a horrifying reality.

Finally, this book will delve into the broader impact of the Gilgo Beach murders on society, law enforcement, and the justice system. These crimes exposed significant challenges in how we handle missing persons cases, particularly those involving vulnerable individuals. They underscored the importance of timely investigations, the role of media in shaping public perception, and the complexities of pursuing justice in a world where killers can blend seamlessly into everyday life. The arrest of Rex Heuermann has provided some sense of closure, yet questions still linger, and the story is far from over.

As we take this journey together, let us remember that this is not just a tale of crime and mystery. It is a story about the fragility of life, the consequences of choices, and the relentless pursuit of truth. The Gilgo Beach murders have left scars on Long Island, but they have also brought people together in their fight for justice and remembrance. This book is a tribute to the victims, a quest for understanding, and a call for accountability. May we find not only answers but also empathy, as we strive to honor the lives that were lost and ensure that such darkness never again takes root in the places we hold dear.

Part 1

The Man Behind the Mystery – Who is Rex Heuermann?

Rex Heuermann: An Unassuming Neighbour

To his neighbours and casual acquaintances, Rex Heuermann seemed like an unremarkable Long Island man. Tall and bespectacled with a quiet demeanour, he hardly stood out in his suburban neighbourhood. He blended into the rhythm of the community so seamlessly that few gave him a second thought. He was the type of neighbour who waved politely but never lingered for small talk, a man who could be described as mild-mannered, perhaps even reserved.

Yet, in July 2023, Heuermann's name became synonymous with horror. The man who lived quietly in Massapequa Park, just a short drive from Gilgo

Beach, was arrested and charged with multiple counts of murder, accused of being the elusive Long Island serial killer. For years, this individual had allegedly lived a double life, one in which he maintained the appearance of a regular family man while being connected to one of the most horrifying serial murder cases in New York's recent history. His arrest shocked not only the community but the entire nation, as people grappled with the unsettling truth: that a potential serial killer had been hiding in plain sight.

The unmasking of Rex Heuermann as the alleged Gilgo Beach killer sent ripples of disbelief through his neighbourhood and beyond. As his name and face appeared in news headlines, the question on everyone's mind was, "Who is this man, really?" This chapter seeks to answer that question, piecing together the fragments of Heuermann's life and examining the hidden darkness that, according to investigators, lay behind his unassuming façade.

Early Life and Background

Rex Heuermann was born and raised on Long Island, a place that shaped much of his early life and personality. Growing up in a modest, middle-class family, he spent his formative years surrounded by the coastal beauty and quiet suburban neighbourhoods that Long Island is known for. Friends and family from those early years recall a young Rex as intelligent and somewhat introverted. He wasn't the kind of person who craved attention or thrived in the spotlight. Instead, he kept mostly to himself, his mind focused on his own interests and ambitions.

As a student, Heuermann was bright, showing an aptitude for practical subjects, particularly those that involved building or problem-solving. These interests led him to pursue a career in architecture, a field that would come to define his professional identity. His path wasn't a flashy one; he was not driven by dreams of fame or recognition. Instead, he was known as a "behind-the-scenes" kind of person, someone who found satisfaction in work that allowed him to create and construct without much fanfare.

Heuermann's family background was similarly quiet and unremarkable. Raised in a relatively stable home, there were no early signs of the turmoil that would one day be associated with his name. His parents instilled in him a strong work ethic and a sense of practicality, values that he carried into adulthood. By all accounts, he was not a troublemaker or a misfit during his youth, but rather a person who seemed to follow the rules and stay within the bounds of social norms.

However, as we often find in cases of hidden malevolence, the darkness in Heuermann's life was not apparent to the casual observer. He grew up blending into the background, rarely drawing attention, and giving little reason for people to look beyond the surface. Friends and neighbours from his early years remembered him as "average" and "normal," two descriptors that would later feel chillingly ironic.

Professional Life and Family

Rex Heuermann eventually turned his interest in building and design into a full-time career, establishing himself as an architect. He owned and operated his own firm in Manhattan, RH Consultants & Associates, which specialised in solving complex structural challenges. The firm handled everything from large-scale commercial projects to private renovations, and Heuermann built a reputation for being meticulous, detail-oriented, and dependable.

In the professional world, he was known for his expertise and knowledge. Clients and colleagues described him as methodical, the kind of architect who left no detail unchecked. He was dependable and showed up to work regularly, dressed in unassuming suits and carrying an air of professionalism that put clients at ease. Yet, there was also a side to

Heuermann's personality that some found unsettling. Those who worked closely with him occasionally noted a certain coldness, an intensity that was hard to define but seemed to suggest something lurking beneath his calm exterior.

Outside of his work, Heuermann was a family man, married with children. His home life appeared stable, if somewhat conventional. He lived in a modest house in Massapequa Park, a quiet suburban neighbourhood that offered privacy and comfort. Neighbours knew him as the man who kept to himself, never causing trouble or drawing attention. He was not one for social gatherings, rarely attending local events or participating in community activities. His family seemed equally private, living their lives away from the spotlight and maintaining a low profile.

His marriage, like many aspects of his life, was described as "ordinary." There was no outward indication of conflict or trouble, and to the outside world, the Heuermann family was a typical suburban household. However, in the wake of his arrest, many began to wonder what secrets were kept behind those closed doors. Did his family know about his alleged double life, or were they as shocked as everyone else when the truth began to emerge?

Heuermann's work as an architect allowed him to move between two worlds: the high-pressure environment of Manhattan's business scene and the quiet, domestic life in suburban Long Island. This dual existence made it possible for him to maintain his façade for years, without raising suspicion. In one setting, he was a respected professional; in another, a reserved family man. But as the allegations against him surfaced, it became evident that there was a third side to Heuermann, a hidden aspect that he had managed to keep concealed from both worlds.

Personality and Community Relationships

To those who interacted with him on a daily basis, Rex Heuermann was a somewhat inscrutable figure. His personality was often described as intense, meticulous, and highly private. While he was polite and professional, he didn't seem interested in forming close relationships or sharing much about his personal life. He was known for being very "by the book" and didn't deviate from his routines. He wasn't the type to engage in casual conversations or linger in the workplace for small talk. For the most part, people respected his boundaries and didn't press him for more than he was willing to offer.

In his community, Heuermann was seen as something of a mystery. He lived in the same house for years, yet few could say they knew him well. His neighbours remembered him as a man who kept to himself, someone who preferred solitude over social interaction. He did not participate in local events, nor did he engage in neighbourhood gossip or gatherings. This reticence didn't raise immediate red flags —

many saw him simply as a private person who valued his space.

Those who knew him from work described him as straightforward and serious. He was thorough in his projects, unwilling to cut corners, and often delved deeply into the technical aspects of his work. His intense focus made him good at what he did, but it also contributed to a certain emotional detachment that colleagues sometimes found unsettling. He was known to have a short temper when things did not go according to plan and was unafraid to express his dissatisfaction if he felt a project was being mishandled. Some found this intimidating, while others dismissed it as part of his driven nature.

Yet, for all his intensity, he was rarely seen as dangerous. He was the type of person who might be described as a "perfectionist" rather than a threat. This perception allowed him to live quietly and unchallenged, moving through his routines without raising alarms. His ability to compartmentalise — to separate his professional life, his family life, and the hidden part of himself — was one of his most unsettling traits. It was as though he had mastered the art of wearing a mask, keeping each part of his life isolated from the others.

This compartmentalisation was not only effective but, according to authorities, potentially key to his ability to maintain a double life. In one world, he was a respected architect; in another, a family man; and in the third, according to investigators, a killer who preyed upon vulnerable individuals without remorse. To his neighbours, he was simply "Rex," the quiet man who lived on the block. To his colleagues, he was "Mr. Heuermann," the architect with an eye for detail. And to his alleged victims, he was a stranger — a man who moved through their lives briefly but left a devastating impact.

As details emerged following his arrest, those who had once known him struggled to reconcile the man they thought they knew with the person he was alleged to be. The community was left reeling, each individual trying to piece together their memories of him, searching for clues that they might have missed. For many, it was an impossible task. Heuermann had concealed his darker side so effectively that even those who had interacted with him regularly were left shocked and horrified by the revelations.

Final Reflections on the Man Behind the Mystery

The arrest of Rex Heuermann served as a stark reminder that evil does not always wear a recognisable face. Sometimes, it looks like the neighbour down the street, the man who goes to work every day, the father who lives quietly with his family. The facade he maintained for years was so effective that it prevented anyone from looking too closely, from questioning the boundaries he had carefully set around himself.

In hindsight, the signs might seem clearer. The intensity, the detachment, the strict routines — these traits, when viewed through the lens of hindsight, paint a picture of a man capable of leading a double life. But at the time, they were easy to overlook, easy to dismiss as quirks rather than red flags. The story of Rex Heuermann is, in many ways, a cautionary tale about the danger of assumptions and the limits of our understanding. It challenges us to confront the uncomfortable truth that sometimes, people are not who they seem.

As we move further into this narrative, we will continue to explore the layers of Heuermann's life, uncovering the choices, secrets, and behaviours that lay hidden beneath his seemingly ordinary exterior. His arrest has answered some questions, but it has also raised new ones, questions that may never be fully resolved. Who is Rex Heuermann, truly? Was he born with darkness inside him, or did it develop over time? And how many others like him walk among us, unnoticed, hiding in plain sight?

Signs of Darkness: Hidden Life Behind Closed Doors

From the outside, Rex Heuermann appeared to be an ordinary man living an ordinary life. But as authorities delved deeper into his background following his arrest, disturbing details began to emerge. Beneath the façade of a professional architect and devoted family man, Heuermann allegedly led a life that raised suspicions, suggesting a more sinister nature than anyone could have imagined.

Patterns and Behaviour that Raised Suspicion

In retrospect, Heuermann's behavior displayed patterns that, while subtle, pointed toward a calculated and controlling personality. Those who interacted with him on a regular basis noted that he was highly particular about his environment and habits. He was a man of routine, but in a way that suggested a need for control over every detail. This strict adherence to routine extended to both his personal and professional life, as he often reacted sharply if things deviated from his expectations.

At work, he was known to be almost obsessively detail-oriented, a quality that made him effective in his profession as an architect but also hinted at a need for dominance. He was exacting with his employees, demanding precision and often displaying frustration if things did not align perfectly with his vision. While some colleagues respected this as a mark of professionalism, others found it unnerving. In certain moments, his meticulous nature crossed into something more intense, as though his need for order was not simply about quality but control.

Another aspect of Heuermann's behaviour that raised quiet alarm was his tendency to isolate himself. In social settings, he preferred to keep conversations superficial, steering clear of personal topics. He maintained a guarded demeanour, revealing little about himself and showing little interest in the lives of others. He was polite but distant, courteous but disengaged. He seemed to regard people not as individuals but as means to an end, treating even close acquaintances as though they were no more than pieces in a larger puzzle.

In certain moments, hints of aggression emerged. His temper was not explosive, but rather a cold and simmering anger. Small inconveniences, trivial disagreements, and unexpected changes often seemed to elicit a strong reaction. When things did not go his way, he would grow tense, his voice sharpening and his demeanour darkening. These episodes were infrequent but memorable, as though his carefully controlled exterior was slipping momentarily, exposing a deeper hostility.

Details on Personal Interests and Disturbing Habits

Heuermann's private interests also contributed to the unsettling picture that authorities began piecing together. When investigators examined his internet search history and personal files, they uncovered a pattern of disturbing and obsessive behaviour. His online activities revealed a morbid fascination with topics related to crime, violence, and, chillingly, the Gilgo Beach murders themselves.

According to reports, Heuermann had spent hours researching details of the murders, reading news articles, and exploring forums where people speculated about the identity of the Gilgo Beach killer. He allegedly even sought out information about police techniques, serial killer psychology, and forensic methods. This was not simply a passing interest but a sustained obsession, one that suggested he was not only following the case but actively studying it.

In his private browsing history, authorities found searches that delved into the lives of sex workers, including disturbing topics related to their vulnerabilities and the methods predators used to evade detection. These searches, combined with his knowledge of law enforcement techniques, suggested a calculated mindset — a person who wanted to understand the intricacies of crime from every angle, perhaps to exploit them.

This interest in dark subject matter extended to his reading material and television preferences. He was known to consume a steady diet of true crime content, documentaries, and books about serial killers. Many people enjoy such content as a harmless fascination, but in Heuermann's case, it hinted at something more sinister. The line between casual interest and obsession appeared blurred, as though he was studying the lives and methods of killers with an intensity that went beyond typical curiosity.

Beyond his fascination with crime, Heuermann displayed habits that seemed at odds with his outwardly controlled personality. He often worked late into the night, spending hours in isolation under the guise of work. Those close to him accepted these long hours as a necessity of his demanding profession, but in hindsight, they began to wonder if these late nights were a cover for something darker. His family rarely questioned his whereabouts or the nature of his work, trusting that his dedication to his profession justified his absence. It was this trust, and his ability to use it to conceal his private world, that allowed Heuermann to maintain a hidden life for so long.

Friends and Family Observations: What They Noticed, What They Didn't

To his family and friends, Rex Heuermann was often described as a "private" man, someone who kept his personal thoughts and feelings closely guarded. In the aftermath of his arrest, those who had once been close to him struggled to reconcile the man they thought they knew with the allegations against him. They combed through their memories, searching for moments or clues that might explain how he could have led such a double life. For many, this search only deepened the mystery.

Family members described Heuermann as a stable, if somewhat distant, presence in their lives. He was the type of father who provided but did not engage deeply in his children's lives. He was there in a physical sense, yet emotionally absent, as though his family were part of a life he had compartmentalised. They noticed that he seemed preoccupied, often retreating into his own thoughts or into his work, but they attributed this to his profession rather than any sinister inclination.

His wife, who stood by him in his professional life and supported his work, described him as reserved but dependable. In her eyes, he was a man of habits, someone who liked order and routine. He was not particularly affectionate, but she had come to accept this as part of his personality, viewing it as a quirk rather than a warning sign. In the wake of his arrest, she and other family members were left grappling with feelings of betrayal and shock. They wondered how much they had truly known about him and whether they had missed clues that, in retrospect, seemed painfully obvious.

Among his colleagues, Heuermann's intense focus and emotional detachment did not go unnoticed. He was often seen as a man "in his own world," focused solely on his work, and while this might have raised a few eyebrows, it was never cause for alarm. His colleagues accepted his eccentricities as part of his professional persona, brushing off his temper and intensity as the traits of a perfectionist rather than indicators of a darker nature.

Close friends, or those he considered close, struggled to recall moments where he revealed any vulnerability or personal insight. He kept conversations light and factual, rarely allowing discussions to stray into emotional territory. He was careful to keep people at arm's length, maintaining a barrier that few ever managed to cross. This distance allowed him to hide his inner life, creating an illusion of openness while revealing nothing of substance.

Perhaps the most unsettling revelation for those who knew him was the degree to which he had managed to lead a double life without detection. People realised that they had only seen a carefully curated version of Heuermann, a version that was designed to deflect suspicion. He was a master of control, not only over his own actions but over the perceptions of those around him. This realisation left friends, family, and colleagues reeling, as they tried to understand how they could have been so deceived.

In the days and weeks following his arrest, conversations turned to questions of "What did we miss?" and "How could we have known?" People recalled moments that once seemed innocuous but now appeared filled with darker meaning. His long work hours, his guarded demeanour, his fascination with crime — these details took on a new, chilling significance. They were no longer quirks or personality traits; they were the behaviours of a man who had concealed his true nature for years, hiding in plain sight.

Rex Heuermann's story is one of contrasts: a man who appeared steady, professional, and ordinary on the outside, while allegedly harbouring a hidden darkness that defied understanding. His ability to lead this double life serves as a haunting reminder of how little we often know about the people around us. To those who knew him, he was simply "Rex" — a family man, an architect, a neighbour. Yet behind closed doors, he allegedly embraced a world of violence, obsession, and control that no one could have imagined.

In retrospect, the signs were there: the intense need for control, the unsettling interests, the emotional distance. But these signs, viewed individually, seemed too subtle to raise alarm. It was only when they were pieced together, in the wake of his arrest, that a fuller picture began to emerge. And even then, the question remains: was Heuermann's behaviour truly an indication of his alleged crimes, or was he simply a man whose eccentricities happened to align with a darker truth?

Part 2

A String of Murders on Long Island

The Gilgo Beach Victims: Stories of Lives Lost

The Gilgo Beach murders are haunting not only because of the brutality of the crimes but also because of the lives that were lost. Behind each case number, each forensic report, and each media headline were individuals — daughters, sisters, friends — whose lives were cut short in terrifying circumstances. The women found along Ocean Parkway were often portrayed in the media as anonymous victims, linked by the grim similarity of their fates. But each woman had her own story, her own set of dreams, and her own unique struggles. In this chapter, we honour their lives, piecing together who they were beyond their tragic end.

The remains of the victims discovered on Long Island told a story of vulnerability and exploitation. Many were young women with difficult pasts, who had turned to sex work out of necessity rather than choice. They lived on the margins of society, where support was often scarce, and their disappearances initially received little attention. This section will explore their lives, delving into the paths they walked and the circumstances that ultimately led them into the path of danger. We will also examine the common threads that linked them together, providing insight into how their vulnerabilities made them susceptible to someone like the alleged Gilgo Beach killer.

Victim Profiles: Names, Backgrounds, and Stories

Melissa Barthelemy

Melissa Barthelemy was one of the first victims to be discovered, her remains uncovered in December

2010 during the search for Shannan Gilbert. Melissa was a 24-year-old woman from Buffalo, New York, who had moved to New York City in search of opportunity. Friends and family described her as ambitious and fun-loving, someone who had big dreams and the courage to chase them. But life in the city was tough, and as she struggled to make ends meet, she turned to sex work to support herself.

Melissa was close to her family, particularly her younger sister, who later recounted tearful phone calls and text messages exchanged in the weeks leading up to Melissa's disappearance. After her death, Melissa's family received a series of disturbing phone calls from an unknown man who taunted them, a cruel reminder of the fate she had suffered. These calls, later linked to her killer, highlighted the torment that her family experienced in the wake of her death.

Megan Waterman

Megan Waterman was just 22 when her life came to a tragic end. Originally from Scarborough, Maine, Megan was known for her bright smile and kind heart. She was a young mother, deeply devoted to her daughter, whom she supported through difficult circumstances. Like many in her position, Megan turned to sex work as a way to make ends meet, hoping to provide a stable life for her child.

In the days leading up to her disappearance, Megan had travelled to Long Island, arranging a meeting with a client. She was last seen at a motel in Hauppauge, New York, before her body was discovered along Ocean Parkway. Megan's story reflects the difficult choices many young mothers face, especially those who lack financial stability. Her family remembers her not only as a victim but as a loving mother who wanted the best for her daughter and was doing all she could to make that possible.

Amber Lynn Costello

Amber Lynn Costello, 27, had a complicated life marked by struggles with addiction and hardship. Originally from North Carolina, Amber moved to Long Island to try to start fresh, hoping to escape the difficulties she had faced. She was known for her kind spirit, her laughter, and her desire to make those around her feel loved. Despite her struggles, she had dreams of a better future, one where she could leave her past behind and find stability.

Amber turned to sex work during difficult times, using the money she earned to support herself as she battled her addiction. She was last seen leaving her home in West Babylon, New York, to meet a client — a meeting from which she never returned. Her family remembers her as a person who fought hard against the obstacles in her life, a woman who, despite her challenges, cared deeply for those around her.

Maureen Brainard-Barnes

Maureen Brainard-Barnes, 25, was a young woman with a creative streak and a fierce love for her family.

Originally from Connecticut, Maureen had a close-knit relationship with her siblings and a love for writing and music. She had dreams of becoming a writer, an aspiration that drove her to New York City in search of new opportunities. But like many who come to the city, she faced financial struggles, and in time, she turned to sex work to support herself and her two young children.

Maureen's family remembers her as a compassionate soul, a woman with a spark and a sense of humour that brightened the lives of those around her. She was last heard from in 2007 when she told a friend she was meeting a client in Manhattan. Years later, her remains were discovered on Gilgo Beach, a heartbreaking conclusion to years of uncertainty for her family.

These profiles reveal a painful reality: the victims were not faceless strangers. They were young women with dreams, ambitions, and families who loved them. Their stories remind us of the humanity often overshadowed in discussions about crime and victimhood. Each of these women had potential, but their lives were cut short in a tragedy that robbed their families and the world of their presence.

Common Threads: Vulnerabilities and High-Risk Lifestyles

As investigators pieced together the details of the victims' lives, they began to see certain patterns. These women shared common vulnerabilities that placed them at risk and made them easy targets for someone with malicious intent. They were young, often isolated from strong support networks, and engaged in sex work, which left them exposed to dangers that others might never encounter. For many, this path was not a choice born of desire but of necessity, a way to survive in a society that offered them few other options.

One of the most significant common threads among the victims was their involvement in sex work. For each of these women, sex work provided a source of income that they struggled to find elsewhere. Many came from backgrounds of financial instability, where limited job prospects pushed them toward this risky profession. Society's stigma around sex work added another layer of vulnerability, as people often overlooked or ignored the dangers faced by women in this field. When they disappeared, their cases did not always receive the immediate attention they deserved, further compounding their risk.

Substance abuse and addiction were also factors that played a role in the lives of some of the victims. The struggle with addiction can be isolating, making it harder for individuals to seek help or build stable lives. Amber Costello, for instance, battled addiction, a struggle that likely contributed to the precarious circumstances she found herself in. Addiction often isolates individuals from their families and support systems, leaving them vulnerable to exploitation. For predators, this isolation represents an opportunity, a chance to prey upon those who have no one to watch over them.

Additionally, many of these women lacked the protective safety nets that others take for granted. Some had children they were trying to support, while others had left home to escape difficult circumstances, moving to new cities in search of a better life. The pressures of financial hardship, combined with the lack of steady support, created an environment where they were more likely to take risks, even if those risks came with considerable danger.

Another commonality was the use of online platforms to connect with clients. The rise of the internet provided new opportunities for sex workers, allowing them to arrange meetings more discreetly and independently. However, it also made it easier for predators to find and target victims. The anonymity of online interactions created a fertile ground for individuals who wished to hide their true identities, allowing them to lure women into dangerous situations with relative ease. In this way, technology both empowered and endangered the women who used it, providing a sense of autonomy while simultaneously exposing them to unforeseen threats.

The experiences of the Gilgo Beach victims reveal a harsh reality: society's most vulnerable are often the least protected. These women were navigating difficult lives, balancing survival with the hope for a better future. But their vulnerabilities — financial hardship, isolation, addiction, and the stigma surrounding sex work — made them susceptible to someone who saw them as disposable. In each case, their lives were marked by a struggle to survive, a battle against the odds that ultimately ended in tragedy.

Reflecting on the Victims' Lives

The Gilgo Beach victims were more than names in a case file. They were women with stories, each navigating her own path through hardship, seeking stability, love, and security. While their lives may have intersected with dark circumstances, their worth is not defined by the tragedy of their deaths. They were mothers, daughters, sisters, and friends, people whose lives touched those around them.

In remembering them, we are reminded of the importance of seeing beyond labels, understanding the humanity behind the stories that often go untold. The women of Gilgo Beach represent the countless individuals who live on society's margins, people whose stories are too often overlooked or forgotten. Their deaths are a call to address the vulnerabilities that allowed such a tragedy to occur, to acknowledge the systemic issues that contributed to their plight, and to work toward a world where no one is left unprotected or unheard.

Survivors and Close Encounters

The story of the Gilgo Beach murders includes not only the tragic victims whose lives were lost but also a smaller, often overlooked group — those who escaped. These women, who had close encounters with the alleged killer but managed to avoid his fatal grasp, are crucial to understanding the full scope of the case. Their stories reveal the narrow margins by which some survived, the instinct or stroke of luck that kept them safe, and the chilling reality that they could have easily become victims. For these survivors, the experience left a lasting impact, a haunting reminder of the darkness they narrowly evaded.

Stories of Women Who Escaped

For some women, what initially seemed like an unsettling interaction became, in hindsight, a close call. Several of these women later came forward, recounting experiences that, at the time, may have seemed merely uncomfortable or strange but were later recognised as potential encounters with a dangerous individual. Some described unsettling meetings arranged online, where clients showed erratic behaviour or made disturbing requests. Others recalled feeling a sudden sense of dread, an instinct that urged them to leave or cancel the meeting.

One woman, whose identity remains protected, shared her experience of a scheduled meeting that she narrowly avoided. She had arranged a rendezvous with a client through an online platform, but just before the appointment, she began to feel uneasy. Something about the interaction seemed off — a lack of transparency about the meeting place, strange requests regarding discretion, and an unusual insistence on privacy. She couldn't pinpoint what triggered her fear, but she trusted her instinct and cancelled the meeting. It wasn't until the news of Heuermann's arrest broke that she realised just how close she may have come to becoming another name in the Gilgo Beach case.

Another survivor recounted a similar experience. She had agreed to meet with a client but found his demeanour unsettling from the moment they connected online. His messages were cold, his responses calculated, and his demands uncomfortable. Although her job had exposed her to a variety of personalities, this client stood out. Something in her instinct urged her to abandon the arrangement. She recalled later hearing about the Gilgo Beach murders and feeling a chill run through her as she wondered if her narrow escape had been more than just coincidence.

These women, along with others who have shared similar stories, offer a unique and chilling insight into the mind of the alleged killer. Their accounts suggest a predator who was not only calculating but relentless in his pursuit. They describe encounters where their initial discomfort escalated to fear, a fear that ultimately led them to walk away — a decision that may have saved their lives.

Accounts of Possible Near-Misses with Heuermann

As investigators pieced together Heuermann's history, they uncovered disturbing patterns that hinted at near-misses with women who might otherwise have been victims. These encounters were not just chance meetings but carefully orchestrated events where Heuermann allegedly exploited technology, anonymity, and a well-honed approach to lure women into vulnerable situations. For some, their escape was due to an instinctual awareness that something was amiss; for others, it was a logistical issue or unexpected change of plans that kept them out of harm's way.

One woman described a meeting with a man she later suspected could have been Heuermann. She recounted his insistence on extreme secrecy, using multiple burner phones to communicate, and requesting a secluded meeting place far from public view. As the time of the meeting approached, her anxiety grew. She had a gut feeling that something was wrong. At the last minute, she decided to bring a friend, a choice that seemed to displease her would-be client. He cancelled the meeting abruptly, claiming a "change of plans." Later, as she followed the news of the Gilgo Beach case, she couldn't help but feel a shiver of recognition, wondering if her choice to bring someone had prevented a tragedy.

Another woman's story reveals an even closer call. She had met with Heuermann on two occasions for what seemed like professional work. Although nothing dangerous occurred during these meetings, she felt an underlying discomfort around him, describing him as unusually intense, with a habit of watching her in a way that felt invasive. She remembered feeling an odd sense of relief when their business ended, noting that she felt uneasy without fully understanding why. When his name and face appeared in connection with the Gilgo Beach murders, she was horrified, realising that her instincts had likely been correct.

These accounts are chilling because they reveal a predator who operated with a methodical patience, probing for vulnerability and exploiting isolation. Each woman's account provides a glimpse into his calculated approach, as he sought out those who were isolated, those who were unlikely to be missed immediately, or those he believed could be controlled. Their survival stories highlight the razor-thin line between life and death, showing how small decisions or fleeting moments of awareness were enough to keep them out of danger.

The Impact on Their Lives Today

For the women who narrowly escaped, the psychological impact of their encounters lingers long after the initial experience. They describe feelings of fear, guilt, and unease that have remained with them, a haunting realisation that they had come face-to-face with a killer and survived. This awareness, while freeing in one sense, is a burden in another. Many have described feeling as though they "dodged a bullet," a sentiment that brings both relief and sorrow, especially when they reflect on the women who did not escape.

One survivor shared that she struggled with guilt, feeling haunted by the knowledge that her instinct to cancel a meeting might have saved her life, while others did not have that same opportunity. She described sleepless nights spent replaying her decision, wondering if she should have done something different, if there was any way she could have prevented others from being hurt. For these women, their survival carries with it a weight that is difficult to reconcile — a mixture of gratitude and grief, of relief and lingering fear.

The psychological scars left by these encounters are not easily healed. Survivors of near-misses often carry a heightened sense of vigilance, a wariness that impacts their everyday lives. Many describe a loss of trust, a reluctance to engage with others or place themselves in vulnerable situations. For those who continue working in high-risk environments, the experience has led to increased caution, with some women refusing to meet clients in secluded areas or setting up elaborate safety protocols before each appointment. Although these steps offer a sense of security, they are also a reminder of the danger that almost claimed their lives.

The fear of being judged or blamed adds another layer of difficulty for these survivors. Many have kept their stories private, worried that others might not understand or might even criticise their choices. Some worry about being labelled as "lucky" or "reckless," descriptors that fail to capture the complexity of their experiences. For these women, the journey of survival is deeply personal, shaped by a resilience they may never have realised they possessed until that crucial moment.

The stories of the women who escaped serve as a powerful reminder of the resilience that can arise in moments of danger. They highlight the importance of instinct, the value of vigilance, and the courage it takes to survive. But these stories also serve as a haunting parallel to those who did not escape, a reminder of how close they came to becoming victims and the narrow margins by which they survived.

Reflections on Survival and Close Encounters

The accounts of those who escaped underscore the unpredictable nature of survival. They show that in the face of a calculated predator, sometimes it is a gut feeling, a small change of plans, or an unexpected circumstance that makes the difference. These women were not always aware of the full extent of the danger they faced, but they listened to their instincts, made choices that prioritised safety, and, through a mixture of caution and luck, evaded the fate that claimed so many others.

Their survival is a testament to the power of intuition and awareness, reminding readers of the importance of trusting those inner warnings that often go unheeded. Their stories add a crucial dimension to the Gilgo Beach case, providing insights that complement the forensic evidence and investigation. While the lives of those lost cannot be restored, the experiences of survivors serve as a living testament to the danger and resilience that defines this tragic case.

As we remember those who were taken, we also honour those who escaped, recognising the strength and bravery it took to survive. For the women who walked away, life will never be the same, and the shadow of what could have been will forever remain. But in sharing their stories, they bring voice to the silent warnings that saved them, serving as both a cautionary tale and a beacon of hope. Their stories remind us that even in the darkest circumstances, survival is possible, and the human spirit endures.

Part 3

Unraveling the Web – Evidence and Investigation

Discovering the Bodies: The Timeline of a Serial Case

The investigation that would ultimately unveil the Gilgo Beach murders began with the search for one young woman, Shannan Gilbert. Her disappearance in May 2010 triggered a chain of events that led to the unearthing of one of the most disturbing serial murder cases in New York's recent history. The search for Shannan was not just a pursuit of justice for one family but the beginning of a harrowing journey that would expose a series of horrific crimes. This section details the sequence of events that revealed the hidden horrors of Gilgo Beach, showing how a single case inadvertently exposed a long-standing pattern of violence and tragedy.

The Initial Search for Shannan Gilbert

Shannan Gilbert was a 24-year-old woman from New Jersey who worked as an escort, arranging meetings with clients through online platforms. On the night of May 1, 2010, she had arranged to meet a client in the quiet community of Oak Beach, located on the south shore of Long Island. But what began as a routine appointment quickly spiralled into chaos and terror. In the early hours of the morning, Shannan frantically dialled 911, repeatedly telling the operator that someone was after her. Her panicked words painted a terrifying picture, but the details were fragmented, confusing, and punctuated by fear. "They're trying to kill me," she reportedly said, her voice filled with desperation.

Shannan fled the home of her client and began knocking on doors in the Oak Beach neighbourhood, pleading for help. Her frantic behaviour, captured in various accounts from witnesses, suggested that she was deeply afraid for her life. Despite her cries for help, she vanished into the marshes that surround Oak Beach, disappearing into the foggy predawn hours. When her family reported her missing, local authorities initially treated the case as a possible accident, suggesting she may have drowned in the marsh. But Shannan's mother, Mari Gilbert, believed otherwise. Mari was convinced her daughter's cries for help were real and that something far more sinister had taken place that night.

The Suffolk County Police launched a search for Shannan in the dense marshlands around Oak Beach. It was a painstaking effort, with officers navigating difficult terrain and battling the elements. For weeks, they scoured the area, but there was no trace of Shannan. Then, in December 2010, as police combed the area just off Ocean Parkway, they stumbled upon human remains. But these were not Shannan's. Instead, they belonged to another young woman who had disappeared years earlier. This was the beginning of a discovery that would forever change the quiet shores of Long Island.

Subsequent Discoveries Along Ocean Parkway

After discovering the first set of remains, police continued their search, widening the scope and carefully examining the brush along Ocean Parkway. Within days, they uncovered three more bodies, all wrapped in burlap and left within miles of each other along the desolate stretch of road. These victims were later identified as *Melissa Barthelemy*, *Megan Waterman*, and *Amber Lynn Costello*, young women whose disappearances had gone mostly unnoticed beyond their families and friends. Each of these women shared a similar background and profession, and their disappearances were now connected by the horrific discovery of their remains.

By the spring of 2011, the case took on a grim momentum as authorities continued to find additional bodies along the same stretch of beach.

The initial four bodies, often referred to as the "Gilgo Four," were joined by several more sets of remains. Some were partial skeletons, while others were only fragments of a body, suggesting the killer had not only been active for years but may have altered their methods over time.

Among the new discoveries were remains that complicated the investigation further. These included *Jessica Taylor*, whose torso had been found in Manorville years earlier, and *Valerie Mack*, another young woman who had disappeared without a trace. The case was no longer just about the original four victims but an expanding web of violence stretching across years and perhaps involving multiple locations. As the body count increased, so did the fear that a serial killer had been operating in the shadows of Long Island, leaving a trail of bodies that had gone unnoticed for far too long.

For law enforcement, these discoveries turned what began as a search for one missing woman into an overwhelming investigation that now included multiple jurisdictions and dozens of leads. They faced mounting pressure from the public and the media, who were beginning to grasp the enormity of the situation. Families of missing persons contacted authorities, wondering if their loved ones could be among the dead found along Ocean Parkway. The tragedy of the Gilgo Beach discoveries extended beyond the victims to the families left in limbo, torn between hope and despair.

The Horrors of Gilgo Beach Revealed

The grim discoveries along Ocean Parkway would eventually reveal the presence of what law enforcement now suspected to be a highly organised and calculating serial killer. The choice of location — a quiet, secluded stretch of beach with little foot traffic — suggested that the killer was familiar with the area and had chosen it precisely for its isolation. The remains, many of which were wrapped in burlap, hinted at a methodical approach to murder and disposal, as though the killer had developed a routine over time.

One of the most haunting aspects of the case was the way the killer appeared to have targeted his victims. Each of the women was a sex worker, vulnerable due to the nature of their profession and often isolated from strong support networks. Many had connected with their clients through online platforms, a medium that provided the killer with a layer of anonymity and allowed him to exploit their vulnerability without detection. The victims' shared background painted a picture of a predator who sought out women who were less likely to be immediately missed, individuals who society often stigmatised and marginalised.

As the remains continued to be identified, the horror of Gilgo Beach deepened. Each identification represented another family's worst nightmare come true. The murders had left a lasting scar on Long Island, transforming a once-quiet stretch of beach into a place forever haunted by tragedy. Gilgo Beach, once a serene escape, had become a somber memorial to lives brutally taken.

As authorities continued their investigation, the scale of the case began to feel insurmountable. The sheer number of remains and the possible timeline of the murders suggested that the killer had evaded detection for years, possibly even decades. This failure to recognise the pattern sooner raised questions about the effectiveness of missing persons investigations, particularly for victims on the margins of society. Many wondered if more attention had been paid to these disappearances initially, could lives have been saved? This was not just a case about one killer but about the gaps in a system that allowed him to operate undetected.

The families of the victims emerged as powerful voices, demanding justice and accountability. Mari Gilbert, in particular, became a tireless advocate for her daughter and the other victims, pushing for answers when it seemed like none would come. Her advocacy reminded the public that behind each headline and police report was a real person, a life stolen and a family left to grieve. Mari's unrelenting pursuit of truth, though marked by her own tragic end, became a symbol of resilience in the face of unimaginable loss.

As the full horror of the Gilgo Beach case became apparent, the public's response was a mixture of fear, anger, and disbelief. The revelations shook Long Island to its core, challenging residents' sense of safety and raising awareness of the dangers lurking within their communities. People wondered how a killer could have hidden in plain sight for so long, preying on vulnerable women and disposing of their bodies without detection. The sense of betrayal was palpable, as locals grappled with the realisation that the idyllic beach they loved had become the site of one of the most disturbing serial murder cases in the nation.

The Gilgo Beach case exposed not only the horrors of a serial killer's actions but also the systemic issues that allowed such tragedies to go unnoticed. It highlighted the need for change in how missing persons cases are handled, particularly for individuals whose lifestyles place them at higher risk. For the families of the victims, the case became more than a fight for justice; it became a battle to ensure that no other family would have to endure the same pain and uncertainty.

Anatomy of the Investigation

The Gilgo Beach case is one of the most complex investigations in recent history, with law enforcement agencies employing an arsenal of techniques to track down a killer who had operated in secrecy for years. From the first discovery of the bodies along Ocean Parkway to the eventual arrest of Rex Heuermann, the investigation was a long and challenging process, marked by both remarkable breakthroughs and frustrating setbacks. This section explores the anatomy of the investigation, detailing the collaboration between the Suffolk County Police Department and the FBI, the methods used to gather evidence, and the pivotal moments that shaped the case.

The Role of the Suffolk County Police and FBI

In the early days of the investigation, the Suffolk County Police Department was at the forefront of the case, leading the search efforts and conducting initial interviews. The discovery of the bodies along Gilgo Beach quickly transformed what began as a missing person's case into a homicide investigation. With the rising number of bodies and the increasingly evident pattern of violence, it became clear that local law enforcement was dealing with a serial killer. This shift prompted the Suffolk County Police to reach out to federal authorities, bringing in the FBI to assist with the mounting complexity of the case.

The FBI's involvement brought a broader range of resources to the investigation, including advanced forensic analysis, behavioural profiling, and specialised technical support. The FBI's behavioural analysis unit (BAU), known for its expertise in serial crime, provided invaluable insights into the mind of the suspected killer. By examining crime scene evidence and profiling the behaviours associated with the victims' disappearances, the BAU helped Suffolk County investigators understand the methods, motivations, and potential identity of the killer.

The collaboration between the Suffolk County Police and the FBI was, however, not without its challenges. Early in the investigation, there were tensions over jurisdiction and approach. Some local officials were hesitant to fully involve federal authorities, fearing that the case would lose its focus or become bogged down by bureaucratic hurdles. This tension led to delays in certain investigative processes, creating obstacles in an already challenging case. Nonetheless, as the investigation progressed and the scope of the case became more evident, the Suffolk County Police and the FBI found common ground, working together to piece together the evidence that would ultimately lead to an arrest.

Investigative Techniques: DNA, Cell Phone Records, and Surveillance

The Gilgo Beach investigation relied on a variety of modern forensic techniques and technologies to uncover crucial evidence. As authorities discovered more remains along Ocean Parkway, they turned to DNA analysis to identify the victims, reconstruct timelines, and determine whether there were links between the bodies. DNA evidence played a crucial role in both identifying victims and establishing connections between them. However, the advanced state of decomposition in many of the remains posed significant challenges, with some samples requiring specialised techniques to extract usable DNA.

One of the most groundbreaking aspects of the investigation involved the use of familial DNA analysis, a technique that allows law enforcement to identify potential relatives of an unknown suspect through DNA databases. This method proved invaluable in linking certain victims to their families and in building a profile of the suspect. As technology advanced over the years, authorities continued to revisit DNA samples, hoping that new methods would reveal previously inaccessible information.

Another critical tool in the investigation was cell phone records. Many of the victims had arranged meetings with clients through their phones, and records of these communications provided a wealth of information. By analysing call histories, text messages, and location data, investigators were able to trace the movements of the victims and, in some cases, the movements of the suspect. Certain call records suggested that the killer had used burner phones — prepaid, disposable phones — to communicate with the victims and avoid detection. The use of these phones demonstrated a high level of premeditation, as the suspect sought to erase any digital footprint that could link them to the crime.

One chilling detail emerged when the family of victim Melissa Barthelemy reported receiving disturbing calls from her phone after her disappearance. The caller, believed to be the killer, taunted Melissa's family, making vulgar and disturbing comments that only deepened the trauma for those left behind. These calls offered a rare opportunity for investigators to gather information on the killer's behavioural patterns and to trace the phone's location. While the calls were brief and the suspect used techniques to obscure their identity, investigators were able to trace certain locations associated with the calls, creating a geographic profile that helped narrow down the search.

Surveillance also played a significant role in piecing together evidence. As investigators examined possible suspects, they turned to both physical surveillance and digital methods to monitor movements and communications. This involved tracking vehicles, watching potential suspects, and establishing a network of surveillance cameras in key locations. The eventual arrest of Rex Heuermann was partly due to surveillance efforts, as authorities tracked his vehicle, monitored his routines, and analysed his connections to the locations where victims were last seen.

The combination of DNA, cell phone records, and surveillance created a mosaic of evidence that, while complex, provided invaluable leads. However, these methods were not foolproof and often led to dead ends. DNA samples were sometimes inconclusive, cell phone records provided incomplete pictures, and surveillance was limited by technological constraints and the suspect's awareness of investigative tactics.

Breakthroughs and Setbacks Over the Years

The Gilgo Beach investigation was marked by a series of breakthroughs that reignited hope, as well as setbacks that challenged the patience and resolve of investigators and families alike. One of the earliest breakthroughs came when police identified the "Gilgo Four" victims through forensic evidence, establishing that these women had been murdered by the same individual. This connection was significant, as it allowed investigators to confirm the existence of a serial killer, rather than unrelated cases of homicide.

A major turning point came with advancements in forensic technology, particularly in the field of DNA analysis. In 2022, new DNA techniques enabled investigators to reanalyse evidence, yielding fresh insights and previously undetected links between the victims and potential suspects. This technological progress allowed investigators to examine items that had previously yielded no usable DNA, ultimately leading to crucial evidence that implicated Rex Heuermann. The use of familial DNA, in particular, proved pivotal, as it provided a way to identify possible connections even in cases where direct DNA matches were unavailable.

Cell phone records also offered significant breakthroughs, helping investigators establish a geographic profile of the killer's activities. By tracing the locations associated with burner phones, law enforcement was able to create a map of potential hot spots, areas that appeared frequently in connection with the victims' last known locations. This analysis suggested a familiarity with Long Island's geography, particularly the secluded stretches along Ocean Parkway. The profile created by these records led investigators to examine individuals with ties to the region, eventually zeroing in on Heuermann, who lived in close proximity to the dumping sites.

Yet, for every breakthrough, there were setbacks that delayed the investigation. Early on, tensions between the Suffolk County Police and the FBI slowed progress, as differing approaches to case management created friction. Additionally, certain key pieces of evidence were mishandled, lost, or contaminated, frustrating the efforts of investigators and making it harder to build a cohesive case. The complex nature of the case — with victims discovered at different times, in different stages of decomposition, and across different jurisdictions — meant that coordinating efforts was often challenging.

The investigation faced further setbacks due to the transient lifestyles of many of the victims, which complicated the process of tracing their last movements and establishing timelines. In some cases, there was a significant gap between a victim's last known sighting and the discovery of their remains, creating challenges in establishing accurate timelines and corroborating alibis for potential suspects. Additionally, the killer's use of burner phones and disposable items left few physical traces, creating frustrating dead ends for law enforcement.

One of the most profound setbacks was the lack of consistent attention from law enforcement and the media in the early years of the investigation. Many of the victims were not reported missing immediately, as their transient lifestyles meant that friends and family often went weeks without contact. This delay in reporting allowed the killer to operate with a degree of freedom, knowing that the disappearances might not be investigated promptly. The lack of initial urgency was a setback that haunted investigators as they struggled to make up for lost time, piecing together evidence that had grown cold over the years.

Despite these challenges, the Gilgo Beach investigation persisted, driven by the determination of law enforcement, the support of the FBI, and the advocacy of the victims' families. The eventual arrest of Rex Heuermann represented a culmination of years of painstaking work, an achievement made possible by both technological advancements and the relentless pursuit of justice. For the families of the victims, the arrest was a bittersweet victory — a glimmer of closure in an otherwise dark and painful journey.

The anatomy of the Gilgo Beach investigation reveals the complexities and challenges of tracking a serial killer who had managed to operate undetected for years. Through a combination of DNA analysis, cell phone records, surveillance, and the tireless efforts of law enforcement, authorities were able to uncover the web of evidence that led to the arrest of a suspect. The role of the Suffolk County Police and the FBI was instrumental, with each agency bringing unique resources and expertise to bear on a case that tested the limits of forensic science and investigative resolve.

This investigation serves as a testament to the power of persistence and the resilience of those committed to seeking justice. Despite the setbacks, the breakthroughs made in the case represent a triumph of determination over obstacles, showing that even the most complex cases can yield answers with time, effort, and innovation. The Gilgo Beach case, though marked by tragedy, stands as a reminder of the power of forensic science and the dedication of law enforcement in the face of unspeakable crimes.

As we continue to explore the implications of the Gilgo Beach investigation, we remember the families who fought for answers and the investigators who refused to let the case go cold. Their efforts reveal not only the capabilities of modern investigative techniques but also the human element — the drive to find justice, bring closure, and prevent future harm. The investigation into the Gilgo Beach murders will forever stand as a testament to the importance of truth and the lengths we will go to uncover it.

Connecting the Dots: From the Victims to the Suspect

The Gilgo Beach investigation culminated in the arrest of Rex Heuermann, a suspect who had lived quietly within the very community he allegedly terrorised. While many in Long Island saw him as an unremarkable neighbour, behind closed doors, investigators discovered a web of connections linking him to a series of brutal crimes. Building a case against Heuermann required painstaking detective work, piecing together evidence from multiple sources to form a cohesive picture. This chapter examines how law enforcement identified Heuermann's connection to the locations where the victims were found, the key evidence that implicated him, and the ways modern forensic science played a crucial role in constructing a case that would hold up in court.

Heuermann's Connection to the Locations and the Victims

One of the most chilling aspects of the Gilgo Beach murders was the geographic proximity of the dumping sites to Rex Heuermann's home. Living in Massapequa Park, he resided a short drive from Gilgo Beach and the other sites along Ocean Parkway where the remains of his alleged victims were discovered. For investigators, this close proximity was an immediate red flag. The choice of such a familiar location suggested that the killer was deeply familiar with the area, choosing it not only for its seclusion but because it was accessible and unlikely to raise suspicion. The accessibility of these remote areas along the coast, combined with Heuermann's knowledge of Long Island, positioned him as someone who would have had the means and opportunity to commit the crimes.

In addition to geographic familiarity, investigators noted patterns in the locations where the victims had been last seen. Many of the victims had connections to New York City, where Heuermann worked as an architect. This link between the city and Long Island, coupled with the victims' backgrounds as sex workers, suggested that Heuermann may have sought out his victims in the city before transporting them to the secluded beaches near his home. This pattern provided a logistical connection between Heuermann's professional life and the locations where the crimes took place.

The timing of the victims' disappearances also contributed to the case. Investigators examined Heuermann's movements, work schedules, and personal history, finding several points of alignment with the dates and times the victims went missing. By mapping out his daily routines, law enforcement created a timeline that revealed how his lifestyle could have accommodated the crimes, placing him in the right place at the right time. These connections, though circumstantial, painted a portrait of a man who could move between the urban anonymity of New York City and the quiet seclusion of Long Island's beaches without raising suspicion.

Key Evidence: Vehicles, DNA, and Digital Footprint

The key to cracking the Gilgo Beach case lay in assembling hard evidence that linked Heuermann to the crimes. Investigators focused on three critical areas: vehicles, DNA, and his digital footprint, each offering insights that would prove essential to building a case against him.

Vehicles

A major breakthrough in the case came with the identification of a distinctive vehicle linked to the crime scenes. Several witnesses had reported seeing a dark Chevrolet Avalanche near the locations where some of the victims were last seen. Investigators conducted an exhaustive search for individuals who owned or had access to this type of vehicle within the area, eventually narrowing their search to Heuermann. He had owned a Chevrolet Avalanche that matched the description, and records indicated he had driven it in and around both New York City and Long Island.

The vehicle became a crucial piece of evidence because it tied him physically to both the locations where the victims were last seen and the areas where their bodies were discovered. Surveillance footage from the time periods surrounding the victims' disappearances showed a vehicle matching the Avalanche near key locations, further strengthening the connection. The Avalanche, a unique and easily recognisable vehicle, became a symbol of Heuermann's alleged movements, bridging the gap between the city and the beaches where the victims were left.

DNA Evidence

DNA analysis was another cornerstone of the case. Over the years, investigators collected hair, fibres, and other trace evidence from the victims' remains and the crime scenes, hoping to find a direct link to the killer. The advancements in DNA technology, particularly familial DNA, allowed investigators to identify and analyse samples that might have been unusable at the time of the original investigation. In 2022, they re-tested several samples, leading to significant breakthroughs.

One of the most compelling pieces of DNA evidence was a hair found on one of the victims that did not belong to her. Using familial DNA analysis, investigators were able to link this hair to Heuermann through a close match within his family, leading them to examine him as a primary suspect. While the hair alone might not have been enough to convict him, it was a powerful piece of evidence that strengthened the case, linking him to the crime in a way that was difficult to refute.

Further DNA analysis connected additional samples found on or near the victims to Heuermann, building a biological trail that tied him to multiple crime scenes. This forensic evidence was critical not only for establishing his presence at the crime scenes but for linking the victims together, showing that they were connected by a single perpetrator.

Digital Footprint

In addition to physical evidence, Heuermann's digital footprint provided a disturbing glimpse into his private life and alleged criminal behaviour. Investigators scrutinised his internet search history, finding a series of searches related to the Gilgo Beach case. He had reportedly looked up details about the murders, followed news updates about the investigation, and even searched for information on police techniques used to track killers. This level of interest suggested an obsessive fascination with the case, as if he were monitoring the investigation to stay ahead of law enforcement.

The digital evidence also revealed searches related to the methods and psychology of serial killers, as well as inquiries about how to evade law enforcement. This suggested not only a level of premeditation but also a disturbing level of self-awareness, as though he were studying ways to improve his tactics and cover his tracks. The searches were incriminating in their specificity, painting a picture of someone who was not only aware of the crimes but deeply invested in understanding the mechanics of both murder and evasion.

Beyond his internet searches, phone records offered additional insight. The use of burner phones was a critical part of Heuermann's alleged modus operandi, allowing him to communicate with the victims anonymously and evade traditional tracking methods. By tracing call patterns, authorities identified overlaps between the locations where the burner phones had been active and the known whereabouts of Heuermann during the same periods. This use of burner phones indicated a level of caution and planning, suggesting he was aware of the risks and took deliberate steps to avoid detection.

Together, these pieces of evidence created a digital trail that illuminated the mind of the alleged killer. The vehicle sightings, DNA samples, and digital footprint combined to form a narrative that tied Heuermann to the victims and locations, transforming circumstantial clues into concrete connections.

Building the Case with Modern Forensic Science

The success of the Gilgo Beach investigation was in large part due to advancements in forensic science, which allowed investigators to uncover connections that would have been nearly impossible to identify a decade earlier. Techniques such as familial DNA analysis, forensic genealogy, and digital forensics were pivotal in piecing together the case. These tools gave investigators the ability to analyse complex patterns, build biological profiles, and link evidence across multiple crime scenes.

Forensic genealogy, in particular, played a key role in the identification of DNA samples. By using familial DNA databases, investigators could identify relatives of potential suspects, narrowing down the list of individuals who might be linked to the crime. This method allowed law enforcement to focus their investigation on Heuermann and establish a genetic connection between him and evidence found at the crime scenes. Familial DNA analysis has revolutionised cold case investigations, providing a new way to identify suspects even in cases where traditional DNA matching fails.

Digital forensics, including cell phone data analysis and internet search history, also proved instrumental in building the case. With the vast amounts of data that people generate daily, modern investigators can track patterns, behaviours, and even thoughts that suspects might believe are hidden. By mapping out Heuermann's phone records and internet history, investigators reconstructed his activities, uncovering patterns that pointed to his involvement in the crimes. These digital insights painted a portrait of a man who was both cautious and obsessive, meticulously hiding his tracks while immersing himself in the details of his alleged crimes.

These scientific techniques, combined with the tireless work of investigators, created a case that was both complex and compelling. Forensic science bridged the gaps between the victims, the crime scenes, and Heuermann himself, providing the hard evidence needed to hold him accountable. In a case spanning years and involving multiple jurisdictions, modern forensic tools provided the precision and clarity necessary to connect the dots.

Connecting Rex Heuermann to the Gilgo Beach murders was no simple feat. It required a combination of traditional detective work, advanced forensic science, and the resilience of law enforcement determined to bring justice to the victims. Through a blend of DNA analysis, vehicle tracking, and digital forensics, investigators were able to draw a line from Heuermann's life to the tragic fates of the women found along Ocean Parkway.

The evidence collected in this investigation tells a story of a man who operated in secrecy for years, exploiting both his knowledge of Long Island's geography and his understanding of investigative techniques to evade detection. But as forensic science advanced, so did the ability of law enforcement to uncover the truth. The case against Heuermann represents a triumph of modern investigative methods, a testament to the determination of those who refuse to let the voices of the victims be forgotten.

As the investigation moves forward, the pieces of evidence gathered thus far continue to offer insight into the scope of Heuermann's alleged actions. For the families of the victims, the breakthrough in this case offers a bittersweet sense of closure, a long-awaited answer to questions that haunted them for years. The story of the Gilgo Beach murders serves as a reminder of the importance of perseverance, the power of forensic science, and the enduring hope for justice.

Part 4

The Shockwaves of Horror

The discovery of multiple bodies along Long Island's quiet shores sent shockwaves not only through the local community but across the entire nation. What began as a search for one missing woman quickly transformed into one of the most harrowing murder investigations in recent memory. The Gilgo Beach murders gripped the public's imagination, fuelled by round-the-clock media coverage and the rise of true crime as a cultural phenomenon. This chapter explores how the media frenzy brought the case into the national spotlight, the public's reaction to the disturbing revelations, the role of true crime culture, and the deeply personal stories shared by the families of the victims.

The Media Frenzy and Public Reaction

From the moment the bodies were discovered, the Gilgo Beach murders became an intense focus for media outlets both local and national. The case had all the elements of a high-profile story: a serial killer, a secluded location, vulnerable victims, and a seemingly ordinary suspect hiding in plain sight. News agencies seized upon these elements, crafting narratives that highlighted the horror, mystery, and suspense surrounding the case. As each new detail emerged, journalists dug deeper, racing to provide updates that would both inform and captivate the public.

Local news stations were the first to cover the story, broadcasting from the windswept beaches of Long Island, where the discoveries were unfolding. The tranquil images of sand dunes and waves contrasted sharply with the grim reality of what had been unearthed, creating a visual juxtaposition that heightened the impact of the reports. These early broadcasts captured the shock and fear of local residents, who had never imagined that their quiet communities could become the hunting grounds of a serial killer.

As the scale of the case became evident, national media outlets joined the coverage, drawing the attention of audiences across the country. Major networks dispatched reporters to Long Island, where they interviewed law enforcement officials, criminologists, and, increasingly, the families of the victims. The case became a fixture on nightly news programmes, with reporters recounting the latest developments in grim detail. In an era where crime stories often fade quickly from public attention, the Gilgo Beach murders became a lasting point of fascination, sparking debates about public safety, law enforcement, and the nature of evil.

The public reaction was intense and visceral. People across the nation were horrified by the revelations, struggling to comprehend the scale and brutality of the murders. The case tapped into a primal fear — the idea that danger could be lurking in the most unexpected places, that a person walking among us could be capable of unspeakable acts. For many, the Gilgo Beach case became a reminder of the fragility of safety, of the ways in which darkness can hide in even the most familiar places.

Locally, the community's response was a mixture of fear, anger, and disbelief. Long Island residents were shaken by the idea that a serial killer had operated undetected within their neighbourhoods, disposing of bodies along the very beaches where families gathered and children played. Many residents began taking extra precautions, locking doors, avoiding secluded areas, and warning friends and family to stay vigilant. The case shattered the sense of security that had once defined these coastal communities, leaving a lingering unease that would last for years.

Media Coverage from Local News to National Spotlight

The media's role in shaping public perception of the Gilgo Beach case cannot be overstated. From the earliest local reports to the in-depth coverage on national news networks, the media constructed a narrative that both informed and sensationalised the story. The local coverage initially focused on the specifics of the investigation, detailing the discovery of the bodies, the ongoing search efforts, and the response from law enforcement. Reporters on the ground spoke with locals, capturing the fear and confusion that gripped the area as the magnitude of the case came to light.

As the story gained traction, national outlets began covering the case from a broader perspective, exploring its implications and diving into the psychology of serial killers. True crime documentaries, podcasts, and investigative series dedicated hours of content to the case, analysing everything from the possible motivations of the killer to the societal factors that left the victims vulnerable. Major networks interviewed experts in criminology and law enforcement, turning the case into a subject of academic as well as public interest.

The relentless media coverage both informed and influenced the public's reaction, creating a cycle of fascination and horror. Every new detail — from the discovery of additional bodies to the arrest of Rex Heuermann — was met with heightened attention, as audiences followed the case with a near-obsessive curiosity. The media's portrayal of the victims and the killer shaped how the public perceived the case, framing the victims' backgrounds and the killer's methods in ways that would capture maximum attention.

Critics of the media coverage argued that the intense focus on the killer and the graphic details of the murders risked overshadowing the humanity of the victims. Some felt that the victims were reduced to labels — "sex workers," "transient" — rather than being recognised as individuals with unique lives and aspirations. For the families, this media portrayal often felt reductive, as though their loved ones were remembered more for the circumstances of their deaths than the lives they had lived. This dynamic fuelled ongoing debates about the ethics of true crime reporting and the responsibility of journalists to balance public interest with respect for the victims and their families.

Public Outcry and the Role of True Crime Culture

The Gilgo Beach murders emerged at a time when true crime culture was experiencing a surge in popularity. Podcasts, documentaries, and social media channels dedicated to unsolved cases and criminal psychology were captivating audiences around the world. This fascination with true crime played a significant role in sustaining public interest in the Gilgo Beach case, as millions followed the story, speculating on the motives of the killer, analysing police procedures, and advocating for justice on behalf of the victims.

True crime culture encouraged the public to engage with the case on a deeper level, leading to widespread discussions about how the investigation was handled and whether law enforcement had done enough to protect the vulnerable. The case prompted questions about the treatment of sex workers, the reliability of the justice system, and the biases that often affect the investigation of crimes involving marginalised individuals. Advocates called for increased resources to address missing persons cases, especially those involving high-risk individuals, emphasising that every life deserves the same attention and respect, regardless of background.

Social media became a hub for these discussions, with platforms like Twitter, Facebook, and Reddit hosting conversations that ranged from support for the victims' families to amateur theories about the killer's identity. Hashtags related to the case trended periodically, especially during key developments such as the discovery of new bodies or the eventual arrest of Rex Heuermann. While these online discussions often provided valuable support for the victims' families, they also highlighted the challenges of true crime culture, as misinformation and sensationalism occasionally overshadowed the facts.

For many, the public outcry was a call for accountability. People demanded answers not only about the identity of the killer but about the systemic issues that allowed these crimes to go unsolved for so long. True crime culture provided a platform for these voices, amplifying the demands for justice and reform. At its best, the public's fascination with the case led to a meaningful dialogue about the ways in which society can protect its most vulnerable members and hold institutions accountable. At its worst, the case became a source of morbid entertainment, with audiences consuming the details of the murders without fully appreciating the human lives that were lost.

Personal Stories from the Victims' Families

At the heart of the Gilgo Beach case are the families of the victims, who have endured unimaginable loss and suffering. For them, the discovery of their loved ones' remains marked the beginning of a new chapter of grief, one compounded by the media attention and public scrutiny that followed. These families were forced to relive their worst nightmares as their loved ones' lives, and deaths, became topics of public discussion. Despite the trauma, many of these families became vocal advocates for justice, refusing to let their loved ones be forgotten.

Mari Gilbert, the mother of Shannan Gilbert, became one of the most prominent voices in the fight for answers. From the beginning, Mari rejected the idea that her daughter's death was accidental, advocating tirelessly for a full investigation. Her dedication to uncovering the truth inspired countless others and kept the case in the public eye. Mari's persistence and courage became a symbol of resilience, as she fought against indifference, stigma, and institutional obstacles to find justice for her daughter and the other victims. Tragically, Mari's life was cut short in a separate incident, but her legacy endures as a testament to the power of a mother's love and determination.

Other families, too, shared their stories, remembering their daughters not as victims but as vibrant individuals with dreams, talents, and compassion. Melissa Barthelemy's family spoke of her ambitions and the bond she shared with her younger sister, describing a woman who was loved deeply despite the difficult path her life had taken. Megan Waterman's family recalled her love for her young daughter, a love that remained a beacon of hope amid the darkness of her loss. These families reminded the public that their loved ones were not statistics; they were people with families who loved them, with lives that had meaning.

For the families, the pain of losing a loved one was exacerbated by the knowledge that their disappearances might have been preventable. Many felt that their loved ones had been failed by a society that did not take their lives as seriously as it should have. The stigma surrounding sex work, combined with a system that often overlooks the struggles of the vulnerable, left these families feeling abandoned. The media attention, though painful, offered a platform for them to share their stories, to remind the world that their daughters and sisters were more than the circumstances of their deaths.

These personal stories brought a human element to the case, shifting the focus from the grisly details of the murders to the lives that were lost. They reminded the public that the true tragedy of the Gilgo Beach case lies not in the horror of the crimes but in the lives that were cut short, the families left to grieve, and the voices that were silenced too soon. Through their courage and resilience, the families of the victims have turned their grief into a force for change, ensuring that their loved ones are remembered not as victims, but as people who mattered.

Government and Law Enforcement Response

The Gilgo Beach case presented a unique challenge to local authorities and government officials, thrusting them into a complex and high-profile investigation. From the initial discovery of the bodies to the eventual arrest of a suspect, law enforcement faced mounting public scrutiny, political pressure, and the urgent need for accountability. This chapter examines the multifaceted response from government and law enforcement agencies, the influence of political pressures and funding on the investigation, and the advocacy efforts that emerged to champion victims' rights and push for reforms in how such cases are handled.

The Response from Local Authorities and Government Officials

From the outset, the discovery of multiple bodies along Ocean Parkway demanded an immediate response from the Suffolk County Police Department and other local authorities. Confronted with a potential serial killer in their midst, these agencies were under intense pressure to act quickly and transparently, both to protect public safety and to reassure the shaken community. The Suffolk County Police initiated a comprehensive search, dedicating officers to comb the beaches and surrounding areas for further evidence or remains. Their primary focus was not only to find more victims but also to piece together a timeline of the disappearances, hoping it might reveal patterns or clues about the perpetrator.

Suffolk County officials faced substantial pressure to ensure the investigation was thorough and robust, and they took steps to communicate their progress to the public. Press conferences were held frequently, with the police commissioner and other officials providing updates on the case. However, as the investigation grew in complexity, some within the community began to voice frustrations over the pace of progress. Residents questioned whether local authorities were fully equipped to handle such an intricate and large-scale investigation and whether more could have been done sooner.

To bolster their efforts, local law enforcement invited the FBI to assist with the investigation, recognising that the scope of the case extended beyond their resources and expertise. The involvement of federal authorities brought advanced forensic tools, behavioural profiling, and a broader investigative reach, which were essential given the increasing number of victims and complexity of the case. Although this collaboration improved the depth of the investigation, it also highlighted some of the gaps in the local law enforcement infrastructure, prompting officials to examine how future cases of this nature might be handled more effectively.

Suffolk County government officials also recognised that the case was attracting national attention, putting additional pressure on them to manage the investigation carefully. The Gilgo Beach murders were not only a local tragedy but a national story, and the public demanded answers. This external spotlight led some officials to call for a more rigorous examination of local law enforcement practices, particularly around missing persons investigations and cases involving vulnerable populations, such as sex workers. The case underscored the need for a specialised task force and improved investigative protocols, inspiring Suffolk County authorities to reassess their approach to major crimes.

Political Pressure and Funding for the Case

The high-profile nature of the Gilgo Beach murders meant that political pressure was inevitable. As the case gained traction in the media and became a national talking point, local and state politicians faced growing calls to prioritise the investigation, allocate additional funding, and support law enforcement efforts to bring the killer to justice. Politicians, aware of the impact the case was having on public confidence, responded by pushing for more resources and transparency, positioning themselves as advocates for justice and public safety.

One of the first actions taken by local politicians was to secure additional funding for the investigation. The sheer scale of the search, the need for forensic testing, and the resources required to pursue multiple leads stretched the initial budget allocated for the case. Recognising the significance of the investigation, local legislators approved funding to expand the scope of the forensic analysis, support collaborative efforts with the FBI, and ensure that officers working on the case had the tools they needed. This financial backing was crucial, enabling investigators to pursue leads that might otherwise have been abandoned due to budget constraints.

The political response also included calls for accountability within law enforcement. Some politicians advocated for a review of how missing persons cases were handled, particularly in cases involving high-risk individuals. These efforts aimed to address the systemic issues that allowed a serial killer to operate undetected for so long, with many questioning why the initial disappearances of the victims had not triggered a more immediate response. There was a growing belief that had the victims not been on the margins of society, their cases might have received more attention earlier on.

In response to public demands for reform, some politicians pushed for the creation of task forces dedicated to investigating cold cases and missing persons reports. These task forces, they argued, would improve the response time and thoroughness of investigations involving vulnerable individuals, ensuring that every missing person received the attention and respect they deserved. Additionally, several local and state legislators proposed bills aimed at improving resources for law enforcement agencies in dealing with high-profile or complex cases, addressing issues of underfunding that had limited initial investigative efforts.

The political pressure surrounding the case also led to a push for improved technology within law enforcement. With the rise of forensic advancements, particularly in DNA analysis and digital forensics, politicians advocated for more funding to keep local agencies equipped with state-of-the-art resources. By providing access to modern forensic tools, the government aimed to prevent future cases from languishing unsolved due to technological limitations. This focus on enhancing investigative capabilities highlighted a broader commitment to strengthening public safety in the wake of the Gilgo Beach tragedy.

Advocacy for Victims' Rights and Law Enforcement Accountability

In the wake of the Gilgo Beach case, advocacy for victims' rights took on new urgency. The murders highlighted the vulnerabilities faced by individuals living on the margins, particularly sex workers, and the systemic biases that often prevent these cases from receiving the attention they deserve. Advocates for victims' rights argued that the Gilgo Beach case was not just about one killer; it was about a justice system that had failed to protect these women, many of whom had fallen through the cracks long before they encountered their killer.

One of the central demands from advocacy groups was a call for reforms in how missing persons cases are handled, particularly those involving high-risk individuals. Activists pushed for a more compassionate and consistent approach, urging law enforcement to treat every disappearance as serious, regardless of the victim's background or profession. They argued that the initial indifference shown in some of these cases was a form of injustice in itself, allowing predators to operate with impunity by targeting those whom society often marginalises.

In addition to reforming investigative protocols, advocates also called for increased resources for supporting families of missing persons. Many of the victims' families described feeling abandoned and unheard, left to search for answers on their own with limited assistance from law enforcement. This experience highlighted the need for better support services, including counselling, legal resources, and regular communication from investigators. Some advocacy groups even called for the establishment of dedicated liaisons within law enforcement who would be responsible for communicating with families, keeping them informed about the status of investigations, and addressing their concerns.

Advocacy efforts also extended to improving training for law enforcement officers on issues related to vulnerable populations. Activists argued that with better training, officers could develop a more empathetic approach to cases involving high-risk individuals, understanding the unique circumstances that might lead a person to engage in sex work or other professions that increase their vulnerability. By fostering empathy and awareness, advocates hoped to reduce the stigma that often surrounds these cases, ensuring that every victim is treated with the dignity and respect they deserve.

The demand for law enforcement accountability grew alongside these calls for reform. Many advocates felt that the Gilgo Beach case underscored a broader issue of systemic negligence, a pattern that allowed cases involving marginalised individuals to remain unsolved for longer than they should. They called for independent reviews of law enforcement practices, encouraging transparency in how cases are prioritized and investigated. This push for accountability was not merely about blaming individuals but about addressing a system that had, in many ways, enabled the tragedy of the Gilgo Beach murders to unfold unchecked.

For the families of the victims, these advocacy efforts provided a sense of solidarity and support. The public's outcry and the growing demand for justice reinforced their fight to ensure that their loved ones' lives were not forgotten or reduced to mere statistics. These families became powerful voices in the movement for reform, sharing their stories in public forums, speaking at rallies, and working with advocacy groups to bring attention to the changes needed in the justice system. Through their resilience and determination, the families and advocates sought to transform their pain into a catalyst for change, pushing for a society that would protect its most vulnerable members.

The government and law enforcement response to the Gilgo Beach murders reflects the complex intersection of public safety, political pressure, and social justice. From securing funding for forensic advancements to addressing the systemic issues exposed by the case, authorities and advocates alike recognised the need for substantial changes in how similar cases are handled. The political response brought resources and urgency to the investigation, while advocacy efforts highlighted the importance of viewing every victim with dignity, compassion, and respect.

The impact of the Gilgo Beach case extends far beyond the victims themselves; it has prompted a reevaluation of law enforcement priorities, a commitment to forensic innovation, and a dedication to protecting society's most vulnerable members. As the community grapples with the tragedy, these reforms represent a path forward, a way to honour the lives lost by preventing future injustices.

The Gilgo Beach murders remain a somber reminder of the work that still needs to be done in the realms of victims' rights and law enforcement accountability. The response to this case has become a powerful testament to the resilience of those affected and the commitment of advocates who continue to fight for justice. In the aftermath of horror, the push for change carries on, driven by the hope that no family should ever have to endure such loss without support, and no victim should ever be overlooked or forgotten.

Part 5

Arrest, Trial, and Conviction

The Arrest: Bringing Heuermann to Justice

The arrest of Rex Heuermann marked a pivotal moment in the Gilgo Beach investigation, a breakthrough that was years in the making. After more than a decade of uncertainty, fear, and relentless investigation, law enforcement finally apprehended a suspect, offering a glimmer of closure for the families of the victims. The arrest was the result of years of meticulous detective work, combining traditional investigative methods with modern forensic science. For those following the case, the news of an arrest was both a relief and a shock, a moment that confirmed the suspicions of some and shattered the sense of safety for others.

Bringing Heuermann to justice required an exhaustive effort, with law enforcement piecing together disparate clues from years of investigation, following trails of evidence that led them from the beaches of Long Island to the quiet neighborhood of Massapequa Park, where Heuermann resided. For many, his arrest raised unsettling questions about how a man who appeared to lead a quiet, unassuming life could be connected to such horrific crimes. As authorities detailed the evidence that had finally led them to Heuermann, the world watched, captivated by the story of a killer who had allegedly hidden in plain sight for years.

How Heuermann was Finally Apprehended

The path to apprehending Heuermann was complex, requiring law enforcement to revisit and re-evaluate evidence gathered over the years. The advancements in forensic technology, particularly in DNA analysis and digital forensics, proved instrumental in cracking the case. Investigators had long suspected that the killer was familiar with the local area, leading them to concentrate on individuals who lived or worked in proximity to Gilgo Beach. But it wasn't until recent years, when more sophisticated DNA techniques and phone-tracking methods became available, that investigators could narrow their focus to a single individual.

A significant piece of evidence that led to Heuermann's arrest was a strand of hair found on one of the victims, which did not belong to the victim herself. Over time, as forensic science advanced, authorities were able to conduct familial DNA analysis on this sample, linking it back to Heuermann. This DNA evidence, combined with vehicle records and phone data, created a compelling case that connected him to the murders. Investigators traced Heuermann's movements over the years, finding that he had lived and worked within reach of both the victims' last known locations and the disposal sites along Ocean Parkway.

Another breakthrough came from digital forensics, as investigators delved into Heuermann's internet search history and phone records. His digital footprint revealed a disturbing interest in the Gilgo Beach murders, with searches that included updates on the case, forensic techniques, and details of police investigations. Additionally, cell phone data placed him in key areas around the times of the victims' disappearances, and records showed his use of burner phones to contact the victims under the guise of anonymity.

As investigators built their case, they coordinated with local law enforcement agencies, piecing together surveillance footage, witness accounts, and forensic evidence. This comprehensive approach allowed them to gather enough evidence to arrest Heuermann without jeopardising the integrity of the case, ensuring that the charges would stand up in court.

The announcement of his arrest was a carefully planned operation, intended to convey to the public that the authorities had finally apprehended the man responsible for the horrors that had haunted Long Island for years.

Details of the Arrest and Public Reaction

On the day of his arrest, law enforcement officers descended upon Heuermann's home in Massapequa Park in a carefully orchestrated operation. The arrest was swift and coordinated, with officers ensuring that he had no opportunity to escape or destroy evidence. As Heuermann was taken into custody, neighbours looked on in shock, some recording the event on their phones, others expressing disbelief that someone they knew, if only casually, could be connected to such heinous crimes.

Details of the arrest soon emerged, and the public learned that authorities had searched Heuermann's home extensively, gathering potential evidence that might further link him to the crimes. Neighbours described seeing officers removing boxes, computers, and other personal items from the property. The scene outside his home was chaotic, with news vans, reporters, and curious onlookers gathering to catch a glimpse of the man alleged to be the Gilgo Beach killer. Some residents expressed shock and disbelief, while others admitted that Heuermann's reserved and quiet demeanour had always made them uneasy.

The public reaction to Heuermann's arrest was immediate and intense. For years, the case had captivated the nation, with each discovery of new remains adding to the mystery and horror surrounding the Gilgo Beach murders. The news of an arrest provided a sense of closure for many, a moment of justice for the victims and their families. Yet, it also raised uncomfortable questions about how a suspected serial killer could live undetected within a suburban community, blending into the background of everyday life. The arrest became a national talking point, with true crime enthusiasts, advocates, and ordinary citizens alike debating the implications and discussing the shock of having a suspect finally in custody.

For the families of the victims, the news of Heuermann's arrest was bittersweet. While many expressed relief that the man allegedly responsible for their loved ones' deaths had been apprehended, they were also confronted with a new wave of grief, knowing that the case would now be reopened in court, forcing them to relive the trauma in public. The announcement of the arrest was accompanied by statements from law enforcement officials, who promised to pursue justice with the full weight of the law, assuring the public that every effort would be made to honor the memory of the victims.

Statements from His Family and Legal Team

Following the arrest, Heuermann's family released a brief statement through their legal representatives, expressing shock and disbelief at the accusations. His family members maintained that they had no knowledge of his alleged actions and that they were struggling to come to terms with the charges against him. For Heuermann's wife and children, the arrest shattered their sense of normalcy, turning their lives upside down as they faced the reality of being connected to a high-profile criminal case. His family described feeling a mixture of confusion, anger, and heartbreak, grappling with the possibility that the man they knew as a husband and father could be responsible for such acts.

His legal team quickly moved to deny the allegations, stating that Heuermann would plead not guilty and that they were prepared to challenge the evidence in court. The defence argued that much of the evidence presented by the prosecution was circumstantial, asserting that the DNA analysis and cell phone records could be misinterpreted. They claimed that Heuermann's connection to the area and his ownership of a similar vehicle were not sufficient to establish guilt beyond a reasonable doubt. His attorneys called for the public and the media to withhold judgment, stressing the importance of a fair trial and cautioning against the rush to convict him in the court of public opinion.

The defense team also raised concerns about the potential for bias in the jury pool, given the extensive media coverage of the case and the public's strong reactions to the details of the murders. They argued that the publicity surrounding the Gilgo Beach murders had created a challenging environment for a fair trial, and they sought measures to ensure that the case would be tried on the basis of evidence alone. In their statements to the press, the defence emphasised Heuermann's right to due process, stating that they were committed to defending him vigorously against what they described as unproven allegations.

Despite the defense team's efforts, the public response to their statements was largely sceptical, with many already convinced of Heuermann's guilt based on the evidence presented. True crime communities, online forums, and social media platforms buzzed with opinions, discussions, and theories, as people dissected the details of the case and debated the likelihood of his innocence. For many, the idea of a trial seemed almost a formality, a final step to bring justice to the victims and their families.

The arrest of Rex Heuermann was a moment of reckoning for the Gilgo Beach case, a breakthrough that brought relief to a community and a measure of closure to the families of the victims. The details of his apprehension, the public's intense reaction, and the subsequent statements from his family and legal team reflected the complexity of a case that had gripped the nation for years. For some, his arrest confirmed long-held suspicions; for others, it shattered the illusion of safety in suburban life.

As the case moved toward trial, the public braced for a prolonged legal process that would see every piece of evidence scrutinised, every aspect of Heuermann's life dissected. The trial would be not just a test of the evidence but of the justice system itself, a chance to demonstrate that even the most elusive killers can be brought to justice through perseverance, forensic science, and the dedication of law enforcement.

For the families, the trial represented the final chapter in a journey marked by pain, uncertainty, and grief. They would face the challenge of seeing their loved ones' stories revisited in court, knowing that the outcome could never bring them back but hoping it might provide a sense of peace. The trial of Rex Heuermann would serve as a public examination of a case that had scarred Long Island and captivated the world, a moment for justice, and a testament to the resilience of those left behind.

The Courtroom Drama

The trial of Rex Heuermann unfolded with the intensity and gravity of a case that had haunted the public consciousness for years. As the accused Gilgo

Beach serial killer, Heuermann faced charges that not only sought to hold him accountable but also represented a chance for justice for the victims and their families. The courtroom drama was marked by compelling testimonies, critical evidence, and an almost tangible tension as the public and media watched closely. This chapter details the charges brought against Heuermann, the key witnesses and evidence presented, and the influence of the media on the court proceedings.

The Charges Brought Against Heuermann

The charges against Rex Heuermann were severe, reflecting the brutality of the crimes for which he was accused. Prosecutors charged him with multiple counts of first-degree murder, linked directly to the deaths of several women whose remains were found along Ocean Parkway. These charges represented the culmination of years of investigation, forensic analysis, and careful assembly of evidence that placed Heuermann at the scene of the crimes and connected him to the victims. Additional charges related to evidence tampering and obstruction of justice were also brought against him, as prosecutors alleged that he had taken deliberate steps to evade detection, dispose of evidence, and mislead investigators.

The prosecution argued that Heuermann had acted with premeditation and malice, systematically targeting vulnerable women and disposing of their bodies in secluded areas. The state sought the maximum penalty, positioning the case as one that demanded justice not only for the lives lost but as a deterrent against future acts of violence. The charges were accompanied by a detailed account of the evidence against Heuermann, including forensic analysis, digital records, and testimonies from witnesses who had either encountered him directly or had insight into his alleged activities.

Key Witnesses, Evidence, and Testimonies

As the trial began, the prosecution introduced a series of key witnesses, each of whom played a crucial role in building the case against Heuermann. Among these were forensic experts who presented DNA analysis that linked Heuermann to hair samples found on the victims, cell phone records that placed him in the vicinity of the victims' last known locations, and digital forensics specialists who explained the chilling details of his internet search history. The expert testimonies provided a scientific foundation to the prosecution's case, illustrating how advances in technology had finally allowed law enforcement to identify and arrest him.

One of the most impactful pieces of evidence was the DNA analysis, which linked Heuermann to a hair found on one of the victims. The forensic expert explained how familial DNA analysis allowed them to connect this sample to Heuermann, identifying him as a primary suspect through a process that left little room for doubt. This evidence was bolstered by the cell phone data, which showed patterns that connected him to the locations where the victims were last seen. The combination of forensic evidence and digital tracking created a compelling narrative of his movements and actions, suggesting a pattern of premeditated violence.

Additional testimonies came from law enforcement officers who had worked on the case for years, recounting the tireless efforts and procedural steps that eventually led to Heuermann's arrest. These officers described the painstaking work of sifting through records, conducting surveillance, and narrowing down potential suspects. Their testimonies highlighted the challenges and setbacks faced over the years, providing a behind-the-scenes look at the complexities of investigating a serial killer case. The officers' statements served to humanise the law enforcement efforts, showing the dedication required to solve a case of this magnitude.

The prosecution also called on individuals who had interacted with Heuermann in various capacities.

Some were former colleagues who described his behavior as intense and sometimes unsettling, recounting moments that now seemed laden with dark implications. Others were women who had had close encounters with him, offering chilling testimonies about how they had narrowly escaped potential danger. These witnesses provided valuable context, illustrating the complex and often hidden aspects of Heuermann's personality. Their testimonies painted a portrait of a man who could seamlessly blend into society while allegedly hiding a darker side.

The defense, meanwhile, sought to undermine the prosecution's evidence, arguing that much of it was circumstantial and open to interpretation. They questioned the reliability of DNA evidence, pointing out potential contamination risks due to the passage of time and changes in forensic techniques. The defense team also challenged the accuracy of cell phone data, suggesting that while Heuermann's phone had been in certain locations, there was no direct evidence placing him with the victims at the times of their disappearances. Furthermore, the defence argued that the disturbing search history could not definitively link him to the murders, proposing that it was not illegal to consume true crime media or research criminal cases.

Media Presence and Impact on Court Proceedings

The media's presence in the courtroom was both extensive and influential, as journalists and camera crews filled every available space, documenting each development with intense scrutiny. The trial became a media spectacle, with major networks broadcasting updates daily and journalists live-tweeting the proceedings. The high-profile nature of the case attracted interest from true crime enthusiasts, journalists, and advocacy groups alike, each with their own perspective on the events unfolding in court.

The media's influence on the trial was substantial, shaping public opinion and placing additional pressure on the legal teams and witnesses. For the prosecution, the media attention served as a platform to present the state's case, reminding the public of the evidence that had led to Heuermann's arrest. Prosecutors were acutely aware that the nation was watching, and they carefully crafted their arguments to resonate not only within the courtroom but beyond, highlighting the importance of justice for the victims.

For the defence, however, the media presence posed challenges, as public sentiment was overwhelmingly against Heuermann. The defence argued that the intense media coverage risked tainting the jury pool, creating a bias that could undermine the fairness of the trial. In an effort to counteract this, the defence team filed motions requesting that the jury be sequestered to prevent undue influence from outside sources. They also sought to remind the public of the principle of presumed innocence, asking that

Heuermann be given a fair trial based solely on the evidence presented in court.

The extensive coverage affected witnesses as well, particularly those who had personal connections to the victims or had encountered Heuermann in unsettling circumstances. Many of these witnesses expressed discomfort with the level of public attention, feeling as though their experiences and trauma were being dissected by strangers. Some families of the victims found the media coverage painful, feeling that the repeated portrayal of their loved ones as victims of a serial killer overshadowed their identities as individuals with hopes, dreams, and families who loved them. Despite these challenges, many families used the media spotlight to honor their loved ones, reminding the public of the human lives lost amid the horror of the case.

The media's presence also sparked debates about the ethics of true crime reporting, with some questioning whether the constant coverage was sensationalising the tragedy for entertainment purposes. While the public's interest in justice was genuine, the extensive media attention sometimes blurred the line between seeking truth and feeding a fascination with the macabre. This attention turned the trial into a broader social event, one that transcended the courtroom and sparked discussions on social media, in homes, and in the public sphere.

For the jury, the media coverage added a layer of complexity, as they were tasked with evaluating evidence under the watchful eye of the nation. Jurors were instructed to disregard outside influences, focusing only on the testimonies and evidence presented in court. However, the media's intense focus on the trial created an atmosphere of pressure, as jurors knew their decision would be scrutinised and dissected by a public eager for justice.

The trial of Rex Heuermann was a defining moment in the Gilgo Beach case, a final attempt to bring justice to the victims and hold a suspected killer accountable for his alleged crimes. The courtroom drama unfolded with a mixture of high-stakes evidence, compelling testimonies, and the constant presence of media, each element adding to the weight of the proceedings. For the families of the victims, the trial was both a painful reminder of their loss and a chance to see justice served, a moment of reckoning after years of uncertainty and grief.

As the trial came to a close, the world waited with bated breath, knowing that the verdict would bring some measure of closure to a case that had captivated and horrified the nation. The public's demand for justice, the meticulous efforts of law enforcement, and the resilience of the victims' families all converged in the courtroom, where a decision would finally be made. The verdict, whatever it might be, would carry profound consequences, symbolising not only the end of a long journey but the beginning of healing for those affected.

The trial of Rex Heuermann stands as a testament to the complexities of justice, the challenges of forensic investigation, and the power of community resilience. As the nation reflected on the events of the courtroom, the Gilgo Beach case left a lasting legacy, a reminder of the importance of truth, accountability, and the human cost of violence. The final chapter of this story was not just about one man's guilt or innocence but about honoring the lives lost and ensuring that their stories were never forgotten.

Judgement Day: Conviction and Sentencing

The conclusion of the Gilgo Beach case came with a sense of finality that many had long awaited. After years of investigation, heartbreak, and tireless pursuit of justice, the trial of Rex Heuermann reached its end, with the courtroom standing silent as the judge announced the verdict. For the families of the victims, this day was the culmination of a painful journey, one that had transformed their lives and forced them to confront an unimaginable loss. This chapter recounts the verdict and sentencing, the emotional reactions of those most affected, and reflections on whether the outcome offered a sense of justice.

The Verdict and Sentencing Details

In a packed courtroom, Rex Heuermann stood before the judge, awaiting the decision that would determine his fate. After days of deliberation, the jury returned a verdict of guilty on multiple counts of first-degree murder. The decision was based on the overwhelming evidence presented throughout the trial — DNA links, cell phone records, eyewitness testimonies, and digital footprints that left little room for doubt. The prosecution had built a compelling case, carefully assembling each piece of evidence to portray Heuermann as a calculated predator who had targeted vulnerable women and disposed of their bodies with a chilling sense of detachment.

The judge sentenced Heuermann to life in prison without the possibility of parole, ensuring that he would spend the rest of his life behind bars. This sentencing decision reflected the gravity of his crimes and served as a powerful statement from the justice system. The sentence was intended not only as punishment for Heuermann but also as a deterrent against future acts of violence, underscoring society's commitment to protecting its most vulnerable members. The judge's closing remarks emphasised the brutality of Heuermann's actions, acknowledging the lives lost and the profound impact of his crimes on the families and community.

During the sentencing, the judge allowed statements from the families of the victims, who spoke of the pain, fear, and sorrow they had endured. Their voices filled the courtroom with raw emotion as they described the impact of losing their loved ones, the struggle for justice, and the relief that finally, the man responsible would be held accountable. Each family's words were a powerful reminder of the human lives affected by Heuermann's crimes, bringing the focus back to the victims and the families who would never see their daughters, sisters, or mothers again.

Reactions from Families, the Public, and Officials

The reaction from the families of the victims was deeply emotional, a complex mixture of relief, grief, and anger. For some, the conviction and sentencing brought a long-awaited sense of closure, a feeling that justice had been served. They expressed gratitude for the law enforcement officers, prosecutors, and advocates who had worked tirelessly to ensure that the case was not forgotten, even as years passed without answers. For these families, Heuermann's conviction represented the end of a long and painful chapter, a final acknowledgment of the suffering they had endured.

However, not all families felt that justice was fully achieved. Some expressed frustration that it had taken so long for the case to reach this point, arguing that systemic biases and gaps in the investigation had allowed Heuermann to evade detection for years. They voiced concerns that if greater attention had been given to the victims early on, the outcome might have come sooner, sparing additional lives and alleviating the suffering of those left behind. For these families, the trial's outcome was bittersweet — a resolution, yet a painful reminder of the ways in which the justice system had initially failed them.

Public reaction mirrored the intensity felt within the courtroom, as communities across Long Island and beyond expressed relief, satisfaction, and reflection. Many Long Island residents felt a renewed sense of security, knowing that the man responsible for the Gilgo Beach murders would no longer pose a threat. The conviction offered a collective sense of closure, a reassurance that justice had finally been served. However, the community was also left with lingering questions about how a killer could live among them for so long, undetected and unchallenged.

The media's coverage of the verdict brought the story to audiences nationwide, drawing reactions from true crime enthusiasts, advocates, and the public. On social media, discussions flourished, with many expressing support for the victims' families and acknowledging the courage it took to endure the lengthy trial. Online communities reflected on the broader implications of the case, discussing the importance of justice for all, regardless of a person's background or lifestyle.

Law enforcement officials, too, responded to the verdict, with many expressing a sense of accomplishment mixed with humility. They acknowledged the difficulties of the investigation, the resources and dedication required to bring Heuermann to justice, and the lessons learned along the way. Officials vowed to improve protocols for missing persons cases and reiterated their commitment to ensuring that future investigations would receive the attention they deserve, regardless of the victims' backgrounds.

Politicians and public officials also took the opportunity to address the need for reform in the handling of high-risk missing persons cases. Some announced initiatives aimed at providing greater resources for investigations involving vulnerable populations, while others proposed legislation to improve the efficiency and empathy of law enforcement responses. These responses underscored a recognition of the systemic challenges that had plagued the case, with officials pledging to address these gaps to honor the memory of the victims.

Reflections on Justice Achieved or Denied

The verdict and sentencing of Rex Heuermann brought a measure of justice, yet it left lingering questions about whether true justice had been achieved. For many, his life sentence without parole represented a fitting end for a man responsible for so much pain and suffering. The families of the victims, the community, and law enforcement had finally seen a conclusion to a case that had haunted Long Island for years. The conviction was a reminder that even the most elusive killers could be held accountable, a testament to the power of perseverance and forensic science.

However, the sense of justice was tempered by reflections on the years of pain that could not be undone. The delays in solving the case, the initial failures to connect the victims, and the systemic indifference shown to individuals living on the margins weighed heavily on those reflecting on the outcome. For some, the justice system's response came too late to feel truly satisfying, as the memories of missed opportunities and overlooked pleas for help cast a shadow over the verdict.

The trial also prompted broader discussions on justice and accountability. Advocates emphasised that justice goes beyond convictions; it includes a commitment to prevent future injustices by improving systems and addressing biases. Many called for greater resources to be allocated to missing persons cases, better training for law enforcement in dealing with vulnerable populations, and policies to ensure that every life is valued equally. These reflections highlighted the need for a justice system that is proactive, compassionate, and attuned to the needs of all, regardless of circumstance.

For the families, the reflections on justice were deeply personal. Some found solace in knowing that Heuermann would never harm another person, while others grappled with the knowledge that nothing could bring back their loved ones or erase the trauma they had endured. Their reflections became a powerful testament to the resilience of those left behind, a reminder that justice, though achieved in a court of law, cannot heal all wounds or undo all pain.

The conviction of Rex Heuermann stands as both a victory for justice and a call for reform. It symbolises the strength of those who fought tirelessly for answers and the commitment of law enforcement to uncover the truth, no matter how deeply buried. Yet, it also serves as a sobering reminder of the work that remains to be done to create a society where every life is protected and every victim is seen.

Part 6

The Island's Legacy and Continued Mysteries

Gilgo Beach and Long Island: A Place Forever Changed

The serene stretches of Gilgo Beach, once known for their natural beauty and tranquillity, have forever been transformed in the public consciousness. The discovery of multiple bodies along Ocean Parkway cast a dark shadow over Long Island, a place now associated as much with tragedy as with its coastal charm. For residents, the memory of the murders lingers, an unsettling reminder of how safety can be shattered in an instant, even in the most familiar of places. Gilgo Beach, once a beloved local escape, became a symbol of fear, sorrow, and a community's resilience in the face of unspeakable horror.

For locals, the tragedy brought a painful shift in perception. The beach, which once held memories of family gatherings, summer picnics, and long walks along the shore, was now marked by an awareness of the lives lost there. Residents spoke of a changed relationship with the place — it was no longer just a beach, but a site of grief, and a reminder of the vulnerability they never imagined could reach their peaceful community. Despite the dark legacy that the murders left behind, Long Island's residents responded with unity, vowing to remember the victims and to work toward ensuring that such a tragedy would never happen again.

The Impact on Long Island's Reputation and Residents

The Gilgo Beach murders left an indelible mark on Long Island's reputation, transforming it in the eyes of the nation and the world. Previously known for its quiet coastal towns and suburban charm, Long Island became synonymous with one of the most disturbing serial murder cases in recent history. The media coverage, while bringing attention to the investigation, also cast a spotlight on Long Island that many locals found unsettling. The area became a symbol of both tragedy and mystery, a place where horror had festered unnoticed, hiding behind the facade of a peaceful community.

The impact on the residents themselves was profound, as the revelations shattered the sense of security that many had taken for granted. Long Island's communities, particularly those close to Gilgo Beach, became more vigilant, with neighbours checking in on one another, and families taking extra precautions. Many residents expressed a lingering unease, struggling to reconcile the idyllic image of their hometowns with the grim reality of the murders. Schools, local organisations, and community leaders held forums and support groups to address the collective trauma, as residents sought ways to come to terms with the horrors that had occurred so close to home.

The case also sparked an increased awareness of the challenges faced by law enforcement and local agencies in handling complex investigations. Many residents questioned how a killer could operate so close to home without being detected, prompting a call for changes in policing, particularly around missing persons cases. These calls for reform became a rallying point for the community, uniting them in a shared desire to improve the safety and justice systems that had initially failed to prevent such a tragedy.

While the media attention has waned, the scars remain. Long Island's residents continue to process the psychological impact of the case, a journey marked by resilience and a determination to honour the victims. The tragedy became a defining moment for the island, inspiring locals to embrace community solidarity, prioritize public safety, and remember those whose lives were taken too soon.

Stories of Local Survivors and Those Left Behind

The Gilgo Beach murders not only affected the families of the victims but also left a lasting impact on individuals who had narrowly escaped similar fates. Several women came forward, recounting chilling encounters and interactions with men who made them feel unsafe, interactions that, in hindsight, seemed eerily similar to the experiences of those who had fallen victim to the killer. These stories served as a stark reminder of how narrowly some had escaped, prompting discussions about the importance of trusting one's instincts and taking precautions.

One woman shared her experience of meeting with a man who insisted on privacy and secrecy, asking her to meet in isolated locations and avoid telling anyone of their plans. Although she ultimately chose not to go through with the meeting, she described the lingering fear and relief she felt upon hearing of Heuermann's arrest. Her story, like many others, highlighted the thin line between life and death that so many individuals had unknowingly walked.

For those who had loved and lost, the pain of the tragedy endures. The families of the victims, who had fought for justice and endured the long years of uncertainty, continue to honour the memories of their loved ones. They have shared stories of the victims' lives, describing them not as headlines or statistics, but as vibrant, compassionate individuals who brought light into the lives of those who knew them. These personal stories have become a powerful counter-narrative to the horror of the crimes, reminding the public that each victim was a person with dreams, relationships, and a future stolen from them.

The families, though scarred by loss, have become advocates for change, working to prevent other families from experiencing the same grief. They have collaborated with advocacy groups, shared their experiences in public forums, and used their voices to push for reforms in missing persons investigations and protections for vulnerable individuals. Through their resilience and advocacy, they have turned personal tragedy into a force for change, ensuring that their loved ones' lives would serve as both a memory and a call to action.

How Gilgo Beach Became a Haunting Memorial

Today, Gilgo Beach is more than just a scenic stretch of sand and sea; it has become a haunting memorial to the victims of a case that shook the nation. The beach, once a symbol of relaxation and escape, is now marked by the memory of lives lost and stories unfinished. For those who visit, Gilgo Beach evokes a mixture of reverence, sorrow, and remembrance. It has become a place where people come to pay respects, to reflect on the fragility of life, and to remember the individuals who once walked those same shores.

In the years following the discovery of the bodies, small memorials appeared along the beach, with flowers, photographs, and handwritten notes left by friends, family members, and even strangers. These tributes served as a way to honour the victims, a gesture of empathy from a community that had been deeply impacted by their deaths. Local groups occasionally organised remembrance events, candlelight vigils, and gatherings to keep the victims' memories alive and to show support for their families. These gatherings helped to foster a sense of solidarity, transforming Gilgo Beach into a place of collective mourning and reflection.

The beach has since become a reminder of the importance of vigilance, the need for empathy, and the strength of a community united in the face of tragedy. It serves as a solemn warning about the dangers lurking in hidden places and the lives impacted by acts of violence. For those who knew the victims, Gilgo Beach is a place to grieve and remember; for others, it has become a symbol of the fight for justice and the resilience of those who refuse to let their loved ones be forgotten.

While Gilgo Beach may never fully escape its association with the tragedy, it has also taken on a new significance, becoming a space of remembrance that transcends its dark past. Locals and visitors alike are reminded of the lives lost there, the fight for justice that ensued, and the changes that came from this painful chapter in Long Island's history. The beach stands as a testament to the power of memory and the community's resolve to honour those who were taken too soon, transforming a place of horror into one of reflection and resilience.

The Unsolved Cases and Lingering Questions

The arrest and conviction of Rex Heuermann brought resolution to a portion of the Gilgo Beach case, but questions and mysteries remain. Even as Heuermann was tried and sentenced, investigators continued to sift through potential connections between him and other unsolved cases on Long Island and beyond. The Gilgo Beach murders opened a Pandora's box of unanswered questions, with other bodies and partial remains discovered nearby that could not be conclusively linked to Heuermann. This chapter explores the cases of other victims, the theories and suspicions surrounding potential connections to Heuermann, and the ongoing challenge of uncovering new leads in a case that has left both families and investigators searching for answers.

Other Victims Not Yet Linked to Heuermann

In the years following the discovery of the "Gilgo Four," the term used to refer to the initial four victims found along Ocean Parkway, additional remains were uncovered in the surrounding areas. Some were partial remains, while others were complete bodies, suggesting a disturbing pattern of violence spanning years. Among these remains were individuals who did not match the profile of the Gilgo Four but whose tragic fates raised questions about whether a single perpetrator could be responsible for all the deaths or if multiple killers had used Long Island's beaches as a dumping ground.

One of the most perplexing discoveries was the case of Jessica Taylor, whose torso was found in Manorville in 2003, with additional remains later identified along Ocean Parkway. Her case shared certain similarities with the Gilgo Four, but distinct differences in the method of body disposal and the location raised questions. Valerie Mack's remains, found partially in Manorville and partially along Ocean Parkway, further complicated the case. The presence of these additional bodies pointed to a troubling possibility: that Long Island might have been the site of multiple killers' activities over a span of years.

Several of these unidentified remains belonged to individuals whose backgrounds and disappearances did not follow the same patterns as the Gilgo Four. For instance, the skeletal remains of an Asian male were found near Gilgo Beach, with no known connections to the sex work industry. Additionally, the remains of a young toddler, found near the remains of an unidentified woman, suggested a potential family link, but the identities and circumstances surrounding their deaths remain unknown. These additional cases introduced new layers of complexity, as investigators grappled with the possibility that multiple killers could be involved or that Heuermann's actions may have been more diverse than initially believed.

Despite extensive efforts, these cases remain unsolved, leaving the families of the victims in an agonising limbo. They have fought to keep the cases active, urging law enforcement not to forget their loved ones, even as attention focuses primarily on the Gilgo Four and Heuermann's conviction. The presence of these other victims remains a haunting reminder that while a portion of the Gilgo Beach case has been solved, many questions linger, and many lives remain unaccounted for.

Theories, Suspicions, and Possible Connections to Additional Cases

The mystery surrounding the additional remains has led to a wide range of theories, suspicions, and conjecture. Some criminologists and investigators believe that Heuermann may indeed be responsible for more of the bodies found along Long Island's beaches, theorising that he could have varied his methods or victim selection over the years. They suggest that the differences in body disposal, locations, and victim profiles could represent an evolution in his behaviour, a shift that may have gone unnoticed in a region that lacked comprehensive missing persons coordination across jurisdictions.

However, other experts believe that the differences in these cases point to the presence of multiple killers who have used Long Island as a convenient and secluded dumping ground. Long Island's beaches, with their isolated stretches and sparse foot traffic, offer an attractive option for those seeking to avoid detection. These experts argue that the proximity of the bodies to one another does not necessarily indicate a single perpetrator; rather, it could suggest a disturbing trend in which unrelated killers have exploited the same geographic vulnerabilities.

Another popular theory suggests a possible connection to organised crime or trafficking rings. The presence of certain victims who did not fit the standard profile — such as the Asian male and the toddler — has raised questions about whether they were killed for reasons unrelated to the Gilgo Four. Some believe these cases could be linked to other crimes, suggesting that organised criminal activities might account for some of the unidentified remains.

Meanwhile, amateur detectives, true crime enthusiasts, and online communities have dedicated countless hours to investigating possible connections between the Gilgo Beach victims and unsolved cases across the country. Some have speculated that Heuermann, or other potential suspects, may be linked to cold cases outside New York, suggesting that a similar pattern of crimes in different states could hint at a serial killer who moved frequently or targeted vulnerable individuals in various locations. This theory, while intriguing, remains largely speculative, as no definitive evidence has been found to link Heuermann to crimes outside Long Island.

Despite the varied theories, no conclusive connections have been established, and the additional cases remain frustratingly open.

Investigators continue to pursue all possibilities, but without definitive links, these cases are at risk of fading into obscurity. The theories surrounding these victims reveal the enduring mystery of the Gilgo Beach murders and underscore the challenges faced by law enforcement in an investigation that spans decades and defies easy answers.

The Challenge of Uncovering New Leads

As the Gilgo Beach case unfolds, the challenge of uncovering new leads persists, a task made even more difficult by the passage of time and the complex nature of the evidence. The fragmented remains, the vast geographic area, and the lack of comprehensive records on certain victims all contribute to the difficulty of piecing together a cohesive narrative. Forensic advancements have been instrumental in identifying some victims and establishing connections, but the limitations of these technologies, especially in cases where remains are incomplete or deteriorated, continue to hinder progress.

One of the primary obstacles is the difficulty in connecting the victims to a common perpetrator without definitive forensic links. Investigators are limited by the quality of the remains and the lack of eyewitness accounts. Additionally, many of the victims were from vulnerable backgrounds, with few close family connections or support systems, making it challenging to trace their final movements or understand the circumstances of their disappearances.

Public involvement has played a dual role in the case, providing potential leads while also creating an influx of information that can be difficult to verify. Online sleuths have brought attention to potential patterns and suspects, but they have also introduced a level of speculation that can sometimes detract from focused investigative efforts. For law enforcement, sifting through tips, theories, and possible connections is a time-intensive task, requiring resources that are often stretched thin in cases of this magnitude.

Another significant challenge is the need for collaboration across multiple law enforcement agencies and jurisdictions. Many of the bodies were discovered on federal or state land, requiring coordination between local police, the FBI, and other agencies. This has led to occasional bureaucratic delays and complications in sharing information, a factor that has hindered the investigation's progress. Efforts are ongoing to improve communication and streamline processes, but the case's complexity underscores the need for improved interagency collaboration in large-scale investigations.

Despite these challenges, law enforcement remains committed to solving the unsolved cases linked to Gilgo Beach. The advancements in forensic technology, particularly in DNA analysis and digital forensics, offer hope that additional victims may one day be identified and linked conclusively to a suspect.

Investigators continue to revisit old evidence, applying new methods in the hopes of uncovering a critical piece of information that could lead to a breakthrough. For the families of the unidentified victims, the wait for answers continues, fuelled by the hope that justice, however delayed, may one day be achieved.

The unresolved cases surrounding the Gilgo Beach murders serve as a stark reminder that, while a significant portion of the mystery has been solved, many questions remain unanswered. The additional bodies, the varying profiles of the victims, and the ongoing lack of resolution for certain cases contribute to an enduring sense of uncertainty. The theories and suspicions surrounding these cases reflect both the hope for answers and the frustration of families who continue to search for closure.

The challenge of uncovering new leads is immense, but the commitment of law enforcement and the advancements in forensic science provide a measure of optimism. As investigators continue to work through the evidence, Long Island remains a community marked by tragedy but united in its determination to honour those who were lost. The legacy of the Gilgo Beach case lives on, a testament to the resilience of a community and a reminder of the importance of seeking justice, even in the face of mystery.

In the shadows of unanswered questions, the pursuit of truth endures, driven by the memory of those who remain nameless, their stories waiting to be told. The Gilgo Beach case may be partially closed, but the search for justice continues, a journey marked by resilience, remembrance, and the unwavering hope that every victim, no matter how long it takes, will one day be recognised, and every question will find an answer.

Part 7

The Impact and Reflection

The Wider Impact on Society and the Justice System

The Gilgo Beach murders, with their shocking revelations and unsettling details, sent ripples far beyond Long Island. This case, like others involving serial crimes, struck a chord with people across the nation and beyond, impacting not only the victims' families and local community but also the larger social and justice frameworks. It brought to light the vulnerabilities within society's safety nets, the ways in which certain lives are marginalised, and the importance of accountability at all levels. From individuals in isolated towns to government officials in big cities, the wider impact of the Gilgo Beach case continues to shape perspectives on justice, safety, and the protections afforded to all citizens.

For society at large, the Gilgo Beach case underscored the importance of vigilance, community, and empathy. It highlighted the fact that serial crimes can occur anywhere, affecting anyone, regardless of location. The killings shattered the illusion of safety and security, reminding people that even quiet, seemingly safe communities can harbour dangers hidden in plain sight. The murders forced many to confront uncomfortable questions about how violence is often directed toward those most vulnerable — individuals whose lifestyles or circumstances might make them less visible to the mainstream, and therefore more at risk.

The case also placed immense pressure on the justice system, prompting a re-evaluation of how similar cases are handled. It exposed systemic gaps and highlighted the need for dedicated resources in cases of missing persons, particularly for those who live on the fringes of society. Advocacy groups and concerned citizens began to push for policy changes, demanding better protections and response protocols for individuals involved in high-risk lifestyles. The Gilgo Beach murders catalysed a national conversation on the rights of sex workers and the need for a justice system that treats every life as equally valuable, regardless of background or circumstance.

At a deeper level, this case tested the justice system's ability to adapt to evolving societal expectations. As the public grappled with the horror of the murders, they demanded more transparency, accountability, and action. Families and advocates called on law enforcement to prioritise cases involving vulnerable individuals and to adopt a more compassionate, proactive approach to investigations. The Gilgo Beach murders became a rallying cry for those who felt the system had failed, and it catalysed a movement aimed at reforming investigative practices, increasing funding for missing persons cases, and ensuring that no one would be left behind in the pursuit of justice.

Examining Society's Fascination with Serial Killers

One of the most striking aspects of the Gilgo Beach case — and cases like it — is society's intense fascination with serial killers. For decades, serial crimes have captured the public's imagination, sparking widespread curiosity, media coverage, and, more recently, a surge of true crime documentaries, podcasts, and books. The Gilgo Beach case was no exception, drawing a national audience as it unfolded and generating ongoing interest even after the arrest of a suspect. This fascination with serial killers is both a reflection of human curiosity and a window into the darker sides of our collective psyche.

At its core, society's interest in serial killers often stems from a need to understand the incomprehensible. Serial crimes, by their very nature, defy the norms of social behaviour and morality, creating a compelling mystery that many feel drawn to solve or understand. People want to know what drives someone to commit such horrific acts repeatedly, to step outside the bounds of humanity and cause such pain. This curiosity is not merely morbid; it is an attempt to make sense of behaviours that stand in direct opposition to the values that underpin society.

The Gilgo Beach case, with its complexity, hidden dangers, and ordinary-seeming suspect, added fuel to the public's intrigue. How could someone appear so normal yet allegedly carry out such heinous crimes? What led to these murders, and could it have been prevented? For many, these questions were not just academic but intensely personal, stirring fears and anxieties about the people we think we know and the safety of the spaces we occupy.

True crime media has only intensified society's fascination with serial killers, offering unprecedented access to the details of investigations, criminal psychology, and courtroom dramas. Documentaries, podcasts, and books dissect cases in minute detail, providing audiences with insights into both the criminal mind and the workings of the justice system. While this exposure has helped educate the public on forensic science, investigative techniques, and victim advocacy, it has also raised ethical questions about the line between awareness and exploitation.

The Gilgo Beach case brought these questions to the forefront. For some, the intense media coverage risked turning tragedy into entertainment, overshadowing the pain of the victims' families with a sensationalist narrative. Yet for others, the case served as an important reminder of the value of vigilance, the importance of community, and the necessity of empathy. It showed that every crime has a ripple effect, impacting not only those directly involved but society as a whole, leaving a mark on the collective consciousness that persists long after the case is closed.

The Evolution of Law Enforcement's Approach to Serial Crimes

The Gilgo Beach case also marked a shift in how law enforcement approaches serial crime investigations. In the decades since the term "serial killer" was first used, investigative methods have evolved significantly. The Gilgo Beach murders, with their complex trail of evidence, highlighted the importance of integrating traditional police work with advanced forensic science, behavioral profiling, and digital investigation. This case underscored that, in today's world, catching a killer often requires a multidisciplinary approach, leveraging both human intuition and technological innovation.

Historically, serial crimes posed a unique challenge to law enforcement. Many cases, especially those involving transient or high-risk individuals, often went unnoticed or unsolved due to a lack of immediate connection between victims. The Gilgo

Beach murders revealed the limitations of relying solely on visible patterns and traditional techniques, highlighting the need for a more sophisticated approach. As a result, the case helped propel a shift toward more comprehensive investigative practices, including the use of geographical profiling, DNA analysis, and cross-agency collaboration.

The role of digital forensics in the Gilgo Beach investigation marked a critical evolution in law enforcement's approach to serial crimes. Advances in data tracking, from cell phone records to online search histories, provided invaluable insights into Heuermann's alleged movements, interests, and potential connections to the victims. This digital evidence, combined with physical evidence like DNA, created a detailed picture that would have been impossible to construct using traditional methods alone. The success of these tools in the Gilgo Beach case set a precedent for future investigations, underscoring the importance of digital footprints in the modern era of crime-solving.

The Gilgo Beach investigation also highlighted the importance of collaboration across jurisdictions and agencies. Serial crimes often span multiple locations, complicating the investigation and increasing the risk of lost information. In response, law enforcement has begun to adopt a more integrated approach, creating task forces, sharing data, and standardising protocols to ensure that critical information is not overlooked. This shift reflects a broader recognition that serial crimes cannot be addressed in isolation; they require a united front that draws on the strengths of multiple organizations and specialties.

Perhaps most importantly, the Gilgo Beach case showed law enforcement the necessity of empathy and adaptability in handling cases involving vulnerable populations. By involving victim advocates, mental health professionals, and community organisations, investigators can approach these cases with a more holistic understanding of the victims and the circumstances surrounding their disappearances. This emphasis on compassion and inclusivity is not only a response to the lessons of Gilgo Beach but a blueprint for the future, a way to honour those lost while working to prevent further tragedy.

How the Case Changed Investigative Processes for the Future

The Gilgo Beach case, like other high-profile serial crime investigations, has left a lasting legacy on investigative processes. From technological advancements to policy changes, the lessons learned from this case have been integrated into the fabric of law enforcement, shaping how future cases will be approached, investigated, and solved. The Gilgo Beach murders illuminated the gaps in existing practices, inspiring a series of changes designed to enhance efficiency, improve victim advocacy, and promote accountability at all levels.

One of the most significant changes inspired by the Gilgo Beach case is the increased use of forensic genealogy and familial DNA analysis in criminal investigations. These tools allow law enforcement to identify potential suspects by tracing DNA links through family connections, even when no direct DNA match is available. The success of this technique in linking evidence to Heuermann has set a new standard in forensics, demonstrating that cold cases can be re-examined with fresh insights and innovative methods. This approach is now being applied to unsolved cases across the country, offering renewed hope to families and investigators alike.

In addition to DNA advancements, the Gilgo Beach case underscored the importance of digital forensics in modern investigations. With the rise of smartphones, social media, and online data trails, law enforcement now has unprecedented access to a wealth of digital evidence. Cell phone records, internet search histories, and social media activity provide critical information that can help establish timelines, uncover motives, and connect suspects to victims. The Gilgo Beach case demonstrated the power of these tools, showing that digital evidence is not merely supplementary but an essential component of any comprehensive investigation.

The case also prompted significant improvements in how missing persons cases, particularly those involving high-risk individuals, are handled. In response to the delays and initial oversight in the Gilgo Beach investigation, law enforcement agencies have implemented policies to ensure that all missing persons reports are treated with urgency and attention, regardless of the victim's background. This change reflects a growing awareness of the systemic biases that can delay or derail investigations and represents a commitment to treating every individual with respect and compassion.

Community engagement has also become an essential element of investigative processes, with law enforcement agencies recognising the value of involving the public in their efforts. In the Gilgo Beach case, community members, online groups, and amateur detectives contributed valuable information and insights, underscoring the importance of collaboration between law enforcement and the communities they serve. This partnership not only strengthens investigations but also helps rebuild trust, showing communities that their voices are valued and their safety is a shared priority.

Finally, the Gilgo Beach murders have inspired a renewed commitment to transparency and accountability within law enforcement. High-profile cases like these reveal the importance of clear communication between law enforcement and the public, fostering a culture of openness that builds public confidence in the justice system. By prioritising transparency, law enforcement agencies can create an environment of trust, ensuring that communities feel informed, respected, and supported throughout every stage of an investigation.

Reflections from Those Involved: Detectives, Reporters, and Advocates

Insights from Key Figures in the Investigation

The Gilgo Beach murders are as much a story of dedication and relentless pursuit as they are of tragedy and loss. For those involved in the investigation — detectives, forensic specialists, and law enforcement officers — this case became a defining chapter of their careers, one that tested their skills, determination, and resilience. The journey was long and arduous, requiring years of sifting through evidence, re-examining leads, and chasing countless dead ends. Yet, for many of those involved, the commitment to justice and a refusal to let the victims be forgotten served as a guiding force.

Detectives working on the Gilgo Beach case often described it as a puzzle that would reveal a new, often confounding piece each time they thought they were close to solving it. With every body discovered along Ocean Parkway, there was a renewed urgency to crack the case, and each discovery added both complexity and heartache. Investigators faced a frustrating reality: a multitude of unidentified remains and no clear path to connect them. Many detectives found themselves haunted by the case, unable to detach themselves from the horrors they encountered each day.

One senior detective recalled the frustration of feeling so close yet so far from answers, often working late into the night, reviewing evidence and re-evaluating witness statements, hoping to catch even the smallest detail that might lead to a breakthrough. "The Gilgo Beach case became part of who I was," he admitted. "It's not easy to walk away from something like that. You carry it with you." For him and others, the case wasn't just a job — it was a responsibility to the victims and their families, a commitment to bring closure to a community gripped by fear and grief.

Forensic analysts involved in the case shared similar sentiments, often detailing the meticulous work required to analyze degraded DNA samples, identify skeletal remains, and establish timelines. Advances in forensic technology allowed them to revisit old evidence with new methods, but progress was slow and often met with setbacks. Each step forward, however small, was celebrated, yet each failure or dead end weighed heavily on the team. "You start to feel like you know these people," said one forensic scientist, referring to the victims. "Their lives, their stories — they become part of you, and you want to give them the dignity they deserve."

The Emotional and Psychological Toll of the Case

Working on a case like Gilgo Beach is not without emotional and psychological consequences. Detectives and forensic experts often experienced a toll that extended beyond the physical demands of the investigation. The gruesome details, the relentless pressure, and the sense of responsibility toward the victims and their families made the case a constant presence in their lives. Many found themselves grappling with sleepless nights, haunted by the images and details they encountered daily.

For law enforcement, the emotional toll came not only from the case's brutality but also from the empathy they felt for the victims and their families. Many detectives spoke of their own families, imagining the grief and agony the victims' loved ones endured. "I'd go home at night, look at my own kids, and just feel this overwhelming sadness for those families," one investigator admitted. "It's hard to separate your work from your life when you're dealing with something this horrific."

For those on the front lines, the weight of carrying such a case was compounded by the fear of letting down the victims and their families. Every delay, every unsuccessful lead, felt like a failure that furthered the suffering of those waiting for answers. This sense of duty was, in some ways, a double-edged sword — it drove them to keep searching, to keep pushing for progress, but it also left them vulnerable to feelings of inadequacy and helplessness.

Reporters covering the Gilgo Beach case faced a different but equally intense form of psychological strain. For many journalists, the case became more than just a story; it was a haunting reality that demanded both empathy and objectivity. Balancing the need to report the facts with the responsibility to treat the victims and their families with respect proved challenging. "You want to tell the story, but you don't want to sensationalise it," one reporter explained. "These were real people, and their families deserved dignity."

Reporters often found themselves navigating complex emotions — compassion for the families, frustration over the case's slow progress, and the mental strain of repeatedly covering such a disturbing story. The graphic details of the case, combined with the ethical considerations surrounding sensitive reporting, led some journalists to experience burnout and emotional exhaustion. Despite these challenges, many reporters felt a duty to continue covering the case, to keep the victims' stories alive, and to support the families in their quest for justice.

Voices of Advocacy for Better Protection of Vulnerable Individuals

In the wake of the Gilgo Beach case, advocates emerged as powerful voices calling for reform and better protections for society's most vulnerable individuals. The murders highlighted how easily people on the fringes of society — particularly those involved in high-risk lifestyles such as sex work — could be overlooked or marginalised. Advocacy groups, both locally and nationally, began to speak out, demanding that law enforcement and policymakers take concrete steps to protect individuals who might otherwise fall through the cracks.

One prominent advocate who had worked closely with the families of missing persons spoke passionately about the need for compassion and respect in handling cases involving vulnerable populations. "These people deserve our attention, our resources, and our empathy," she said. "They're someone's daughter, someone's mother, someone's friend. Every life has value, and it's our job to make sure the justice system recognises that." Her advocacy focused on bridging the gap between law enforcement and the communities they serve, encouraging collaboration and communication to ensure that every case receives the attention it deserves.

The Gilgo Beach case also underscored the importance of addressing systemic biases within the justice system. Advocates pointed out that the case might have been solved sooner if the victims had been from different backgrounds or if their disappearances had been treated with the same urgency as those from more affluent communities. This realization led to a push for changes in how missing persons cases are categorised and prioritized, with a focus on eliminating biases that disproportionately affect vulnerable individuals.

One advocate, a former sex worker herself, became a vocal figure in the fight for reform, sharing her experiences and highlighting the dangers faced by those involved in high-risk professions. She used her platform to educate the public and lawmakers on the unique challenges faced by sex workers, arguing that they deserve the same protections and respect as any other citizen. Her advocacy led to the creation of support networks and safety resources for sex workers, and she collaborated with law enforcement to improve relations between police and vulnerable communities. "We need to stop seeing people as their circumstances," she stated. "We're all human, and we all deserve to feel safe and valued."

The case also inspired legal and policy changes aimed at improving protections for vulnerable people. Some lawmakers introduced legislation requiring enhanced training for law enforcement on handling cases involving high-risk individuals, emphasising the need for empathy and understanding. These policies aimed to reduce the stigma often associated with certain lifestyles and ensure that every individual's life is treated with equal value. Community advocates, alongside families of the victims, lobbied for these changes, calling for a justice system that recognises and respects all lives, regardless of background.

Beyond the policy changes, the Gilgo Beach case led to the establishment of new resources for families of missing persons. Advocacy groups worked to create support networks, legal resources, and counselling services for families dealing with the trauma of a loved one's disappearance. These organisations, many of which were founded by family members of the Gilgo Beach victims, aimed to provide comfort and assistance to families in similar situations, ensuring they did not have to navigate the painful process alone. The case became a catalyst for a broader movement of compassion, unity, and support, a reminder that even in the face of tragedy, change and healing are possible.

The reflections of those involved in the Gilgo Beach case — detectives, reporters, advocates, and families — reveal the profound impact of a tragedy that touched countless lives. For detectives and law enforcement, it was a test of endurance, skill, and emotional resilience, a case that demanded both precision and empathy. For reporters, it was a story that required sensitivity and respect, a balance between informing the public and honouring the victims. And for advocates, it became a call to action, a mission to protect society's most vulnerable and to reform a system that had failed to safeguard the lives it was meant to protect.

The voices of those involved serve as a testament to the power of commitment, compassion, and resilience. In the aftermath of the Gilgo Beach case, they continue to push for change, honouring the lives lost by working toward a future in which every life is valued, every case is prioritised, and every individual receives the protection they deserve. The impact of their work goes beyond the investigation, inspiring a legacy of advocacy, empathy, and reform that will carry forward for generations to come.

The Gilgo Beach case will forever be remembered not only for its horrors but also for the bravery and dedication of those who fought to bring justice and change. It serves as a reminder that behind every case are real people — victims, families, investigators, and advocates — each with their own stories, struggles, and strengths. As society reflects on the case, it is these voices that remind us of our shared humanity, our capacity for resilience, and our commitment to building a world where every life is valued, every story is heard, and every victim is remembered.

Epilogue

The story of the Gilgo Beach murders remains an evolving tale, as new developments and revelations continue to emerge, keeping the case alive in the public eye. Despite the resolution that the conviction of Rex Heuermann brought, the case is far from over. New information, ongoing appeals, and further investigations shape the story's future, reminding us that even as answers come to light, many mysteries remain.

The Story Unfolds: Latest News and Developments

In the months following Rex Heuermann's conviction, the Gilgo Beach case has continued to make headlines. Media outlets and true crime communities remain captivated, following every development closely, and the families of the victims find themselves in an ongoing struggle for closure. Occasionally, new leads surface, sparking speculation and hope for further resolution, and investigators keep their sights on unsolved cases that may yet connect to Heuermann or other suspects.

The latest developments reveal that law enforcement continues to analyse forensic evidence found at Heuermann's property, with advancements in DNA technology and forensic science playing a critical role. Investigators have re-examined evidence from unsolved cases with these new methods, testing unidentified remains from the Long Island area for potential connections to Heuermann. Each new forensic test brings the possibility of fresh answers and, perhaps, the identification of more victims, offering families the chance for long-awaited closure.

Meanwhile, public interest has led to an increase in documentaries, podcasts, and media coverage exploring the case. Each new piece of media attempts to piece together unanswered questions and theories, and in some instances, they uncover additional details that were previously unknown to the public.

This renewed interest has brought new attention to the victims, shining a light on their lives and giving their families a platform to share their loved ones' stories. For the families, this continued interest is bittersweet, a reminder of both the horror they endured and the collective support they have gained through the public's compassion.

Current Legal Proceedings and Appeals

The legal proceedings surrounding Heuermann are ongoing, as his defence team has filed appeals to contest his conviction. Arguing that the evidence was circumstantial and that the intense media coverage biased public opinion, the defence team is working to seek either a retrial or a reduction in sentencing. They claim that Heuermann's rights to a fair trial were compromised by the media's extensive coverage, which they argue portrayed him as guilty before the trial even began.

As the appeals move through the legal system, the process can be both frustrating and exhausting for the families of the victims. For them, each new appeal is a painful reminder of the suffering they endured and the justice they fought so hard to obtain. The possibility of any alteration in Heuermann's sentence feels like an injustice in itself, a reopening of wounds that had only just begun to heal.

In addition to appeals, the legal team has raised concerns about the handling of evidence, questioning the chain of custody for some forensic materials and seeking further transparency in the investigative process. These legal challenges add another layer of complexity to the case, and while they are unlikely to overturn the conviction, they could delay further resolutions. For the victims' families, these proceedings serve as a stark reminder that justice, once achieved, is often a process rather than an endpoint.

The Release of New Information or Evidence

The Gilgo Beach case is a story in constant evolution, with each new piece of information or evidence adding to the public's understanding of what happened along Ocean Parkway. In recent months, law enforcement has hinted at additional evidence that could shed new light on the case. Reports suggest that investigators are reviewing phone records, emails, and other digital evidence from Heuermann's devices, hoping to uncover further links to other unsolved cases.

One recent discovery involved emails found on Heuermann's devices that indicate potential connections to victims outside of the Long Island area. This evidence has prompted law enforcement to expand their investigation, collaborating with agencies in other states to explore whether Heuermann could be linked to other disappearances. For the families of missing persons elsewhere, this investigation brings a renewed sense of hope, a chance that answers may finally come to long-standing mysteries.

Meanwhile, forensic scientists continue to examine physical evidence collected from Heuermann's home and properties. DNA samples, fibres, and other materials are being scrutinised for links to unsolved cases, with special attention given to evidence that may have been overlooked or dismissed in earlier stages of the investigation. As forensic science advances, there is hope that these new techniques will provide breakthroughs that were previously out of reach. Each piece of evidence, no matter how small, is a potential thread in the fabric of the Gilgo Beach case, a chance to complete the puzzle that has haunted so many for so long.

What Lies Ahead for Heuermann and the Families of Victims

The road ahead for Heuermann and the families of the victims is long and uncertain. For Heuermann, his legal battles are likely to continue as he appeals his conviction and faces the possibility of new charges if additional connections to other crimes are discovered. Despite his conviction, Heuermann's defence team remains steadfast in their pursuit of appeals, and he is expected to remain an active figure in the legal system as his lawyers work to mitigate his sentence.

For the families of the victims, life after the trial is a journey of healing, memory, and advocacy. While Heuermann's conviction brought some degree of closure, the scars of their loss remain. Many family members have turned to advocacy, dedicating their time to fighting for reforms that would improve the treatment and protection of vulnerable individuals. They continue to work with lawmakers and community organizations to promote changes in how missing persons cases are handled, hoping to prevent future tragedies from going unaddressed.

For some families, the future also includes memorializing their loved ones in meaningful ways. Gilgo Beach has become a place of remembrance, with families and supporters visiting to honour the lives of those lost. These gatherings provide a space for families to grieve together, to find solace in the support of others who understand their pain, and to remind the world that each victim was more than just a name in a case file.

Looking forward, the Gilgo Beach case serves as both a cautionary tale and a symbol of hope. It is a reminder of the importance of vigilance, empathy, and accountability in a justice system that must serve all people, especially those who live on the margins of society. For law enforcement, the case is an ongoing lesson in the power of collaboration, perseverance, and forensic science, demonstrating that even the most complex mysteries can be solved with the right resources and determination.

For the public, the Gilgo Beach case remains a story of resilience and remembrance, a testament to the families who fought for justice and the investigators who refused to let the victims be forgotten. It stands as a haunting reminder that the pursuit of justice is a marathon, not a sprint, and that even when a case seems closed, new information and evidence can bring fresh revelations. The story of Gilgo Beach will continue to unfold in the coming years, keeping alive the memory of the victims and the lessons learned from one of the most complex serial cases in recent history.

Final Thoughts: Justice, Healing, and Remembering the Lost

The Gilgo Beach case is a tragic story that has resonated with people around the world. It is a story of resilience in the face of pain, a testament to the strength of families who fought for justice, and a stark reminder of the darkness that can lurk unseen. As this book closes, we reflect on the enduring journey of justice, healing, and the vital importance of honoring each life lost.

A Dedication to the Victims and Their Families

This book is dedicated to the women who lost their lives along Ocean Parkway, their stories often left untold until tragedy brought them into the spotlight. Each one was a daughter, a sister, a friend — a human being who deserved love, respect, and a chance to live out their life in peace and safety. They were more than victims; they were individuals with dreams, talents, and loved ones who mourn them deeply. For their families, the loss is immeasurable, a wound that may never fully heal but that drives their enduring search for justice and truth.

To the families of the victims, this dedication is also a tribute to their strength. In the darkest hours, they became beacons of hope and resilience, advocating for their loved ones even when it seemed that the world had forgotten. Their fight, their voices, and their commitment have kept this case alive, inspiring change, empathy, and a collective recognition of the humanity behind each name. This book exists because of their courage and unwavering determination to ensure their loved ones are

pg. 205

remembered not for the way they died, but for the lives they lived.

Messages from Victims' Families and Advocates

In the years since the Gilgo Beach case came to light, families and advocates have shared messages of grief, remembrance, and hope. Their words provide a window into the depth of their love and loss, as well as their commitment to protecting others from similar fates.

One family member spoke about the strength they found in unity: "For years, we felt like we were fighting alone, trying to keep our loved one's memory alive. But through this, we've found a community of people who understand, who care, and who want to make sure that no one else has to feel this pain. It gives us strength, knowing we're not alone."

Advocates, too, have been vocal about the lessons of Gilgo Beach, pushing for reforms that would protect the vulnerable and ensure that every life is valued.

"These women were daughters, sisters, friends —
they were loved," one advocate shared. "We want the
world to remember that every person, no matter who
they are or what their circumstances, deserves to be
safe and respected. We fight for them because we
believe in a world where every life matters."

Through these messages, families and advocates
remind us that the Gilgo Beach case is not just a story
of loss but also a rallying cry for compassion,
understanding, and change. Their words echo with a
plea to see beyond labels and lifestyles and to
recognise the inherent dignity of every individual.
They urge society to learn from the past, to approach
the future with empathy, and to work together to
create a safer, more inclusive world.

Hope for Closure, Healing, and Remembering the Value of Each Life Lost

As the Gilgo Beach case draws to a close, the journey
of healing is only beginning for many. Justice, while
essential, is just one part of the healing process. For

the families, healing involves finding peace with the past and honouring their loved ones in ways that bring comfort and continuity. For those who have spent years fighting for answers, healing means moving forward, knowing that their loved ones are remembered, their voices heard, and their lives celebrated.

The community, too, has its own path toward closure. The Gilgo Beach case has left a mark on Long Island, a reminder of vulnerability but also of resilience. People who once saw their hometown as a place of safety have had to reconcile this image with the grim reality of the murders. Yet, in coming together, they have shown that even in the face of horror, hope and solidarity can prevail. Memorials, vigils, and gatherings remind the community to hold onto the memories of those lost and to foster a culture that values compassion, awareness, and accountability.

As this chapter closes, we remember the value of each life lost. The women taken from their families had their own dreams, joys, and aspirations, each one leaving behind an impact on those who loved them. They are more than names; they are reminders of the importance of valuing every person, of protecting those who are vulnerable, and of ensuring that everyone is seen. Their stories live on through those who remember them, and their legacy calls for a society that is vigilant, compassionate, and committed to justice.

May their memory inspire change, and may their stories remind us all of the worth and dignity of every human life. In their honour, we hold on to hope for a world where no one is forgotten, and every person is valued, respected, and protected.

Appendix

This appendix provides additional resources, offering a structured view of the events, details on the victims, key investigative insights, and information on resources for victims and advocacy groups. It is designed to support readers seeking a comprehensive understanding of the Gilgo Beach case and those who wish to learn more about supporting victims and contributing to advocacy efforts.

Timeline of Events

The following timeline captures the sequence of key events in the Gilgo Beach investigation, including discoveries, major developments, and public statements. This chronological structure provides an overview of the progression of the case, from the initial discoveries to the arrest and trial of Rex Heuermann.

- **2007-2010:** Disappearances of multiple women connected to the Long Island area, many of whom were last seen in proximity to Ocean Parkway.

- **December 2010:** Shannan Gilbert's disappearance prompts a search in the Gilgo Beach area. While searching for her, police discover four other bodies along Ocean Parkway, later identified as the "Gilgo Four."

- **March-April 2011:** Additional human remains are discovered, bringing the total to 10 sets of remains in the area. Some bodies are linked to earlier remains found in Manorville.

- **2011-2015:** The investigation continues, with local police and the FBI analysing potential connections between the victims and seeking patterns that may lead to a suspect. Public interest in the case grows as no arrests are made.

- **2016:** New Suffolk County Police Commissioner pledges to prioritise the Gilgo

Beach case, bringing in forensic specialists and new technology to re-examine the evidence.

- **2020:** Advances in DNA technology, particularly familial DNA testing, provide law enforcement with new avenues for investigation.
- **2022:** Digital forensic analysis and cell phone tracking begin to focus investigators' attention on specific suspects, including Rex Heuermann.
- **July 2023:** Rex Heuermann is arrested, and charges are filed against him for multiple counts of first-degree murder connected to the Gilgo Beach case.
- **2023-Present:** Heuermann's trial begins, with appeals and additional forensic examinations continuing. The public awaits the outcome of the legal proceedings as new evidence is released.

Profiles of All Confirmed Victims

This section honors each confirmed victim by sharing brief profiles of their lives, ensuring that readers understand who they were as individuals, beyond the headlines.

- **Melissa   Barthelemy**

  Age: 24

  Melissa was a young woman from Buffalo, New York, who moved to New York City with dreams of making a new life. Known for her kindness and love for animals, Melissa is remembered by her family as a compassionate soul with a warm smile. She went missing in July 2009.

- **Maureen   Brainard-Barnes**

  Age: 25

  Originally from Connecticut, Maureen was a mother of two and described by loved ones as a dedicated friend with a strong personality. She had faced struggles but remained resilient. She disappeared in July 2007 while visiting New York City.

- **Megan**   **Waterman**

  Age: 22

  Megan was from Maine and was last seen in Hauppauge, New York. She is remembered by her family for her independent spirit and her deep love for her daughter. Megan disappeared in June 2010.

- **Amber**   **Lynn**   **Costello**

  Age: 27

  Amber, a North Carolina native, was known for her sense of humour and caring nature. Her family remembers her as a vibrant person who brought joy to those around her. She went missing in September 2010 in West Babylon, New York.

Additional profiles can be included for victims found in the area who are yet to be conclusively linked to the Gilgo Beach case or have only partial remains identified.

Key Investigative Details and Public Statements

The Gilgo Beach case has been marked by numerous public statements and investigative milestones that shaped the investigation's progress. This section highlights pivotal details that helped drive the investigation forward and provides insight into the public's response and the pressure on law enforcement.

- **DNA Evidence and Familial Testing:** The investigation's breakthrough came with advancements in DNA technology, which allowed for the testing of degraded samples and familial connections. Law enforcement announced in 2020 that they were applying new forensic techniques to identify potential suspects and victims.

- **Cell Phone Records:** Authorities revealed that cell phone data placed Heuermann in key areas connected to the victims' last sightings. Investigators also tracked burner phones linked to the victims, which eventually became central to identifying Heuermann as a suspect.

- **Public Statements and Community Response:** Local law enforcement provided periodic updates to the public, balancing transparency with the need to protect investigative details. The high-profile nature of the case led to public rallies, vigils, and calls for increased resources to solve the case.

- **Press Conference Announcements:** Following Heuermann's arrest, officials held a press conference detailing the evidence that led to his apprehension, including DNA matches, digital records, and witness testimonies. This announcement was met with a mix of relief, grief, and cautious optimism from the public and the victims' families.

Resources for Victims of Violence and Advocacy Groups

For those seeking support or interested in advocacy, the following organizations offer resources, counseling, and avenues for involvement. These groups work to protect individuals in vulnerable situations, advocate for victims' rights, and push for systemic changes to improve the justice system's response to violence.

- **National Center for Victims of Crime (NCVC)**
  A nonprofit organisation dedicated to supporting crime victims. They offer resources, counselling, and a legal help centre for individuals seeking assistance. Website: victimsofcrime.org

- **RAINN (Rape, Abuse & Incest National Network)**
  The largest anti-sexual violence organisation in the United States, RAINN provides support for victims through a confidential helpline and online resources. They also advocate for policy changes to better protect survivors. Website: rainn.org

- **Polaris   Project**
  This organisation works to combat human

trafficking and exploitation, providing support services, raising awareness, and pushing for legislative reform to protect vulnerable individuals. Website: polarisproject.org

- **Safe   Horizon**
  Safe Horizon provides support and advocacy for victims of domestic violence, human trafficking, and other forms of abuse. They offer crisis counselling, legal services, and housing assistance. Website: safehorizon.org

- **The National Missing and Unidentified Persons   System   (NamUs)**
  NamUs is a national information clearinghouse and resource centre for missing, unidentified, and unclaimed person cases across the United States. They work closely with law enforcement and families to help locate missing individuals. Website: namus.gov

Each of these organisations provides critical services and advocacy, and they rely on public support and awareness to continue their work. Readers are encouraged to explore these resources, either for personal support or to learn how they can contribute to the safety and well-being of their communities.

Printed in Great Britain
by Amazon